MW00440424

Prayer Works!

by

Robert Collier

All rights reserved. No part of this publication may be reproduced, stored in a retrieval system, or transmitted in any form or by any means, electronic, mechanical, photocopying or otherwise, without the prior permission of the copyright owner.

For information regarding special discounts for bulk purchases,

please contact BN Publishing at info@bnpublishing.com

©**Copyright 2007 – BN Publishing**

www.bnpublishing.com

ALL RIGHTS RESERVED

Printed in the U.S.A.

Contents

PREFACE

Dear Reader:

In his book Effective Prayer, Russell Conwell tells how a small congregation, with no wealthy members and little or no property, built a $100,000 Church on an initial capital of 57 cents—through the power of prayer!

It seems that the people had been giving so generously toward the building of the Church, that Dr. Conwell hesitated to burden them with the additional expense of a new organ. But one member felt that this was showing a lack of faith in the Giver of all gifts, so he asked for and received permission to try to raise the necessary $10,000, on condition that he should not approach anyone for a contribution who had already given toward the building of the Church.

So this earnest member started his campaign. Having nothing to give himself, he had to get the entire amount from others. Nevertheless, such was his faith, that he went right ahead and signed the contract for the organ, giving his personal notes for the necessary $10,000.

The first installment was $1,500, and as the time for its payment drew near, he "wrestled with the Lord" in earnest and tearful prayer. The note fell due on a Monday, so on the Sunday proceeding, he asked the prayer meeting to remember him especially on the morrow. The Bank closed at three o'clock, and he had only until then to find the amount and save his note from protest.

On Monday morning, a working girl who was a fellow-member of the Church handed him a letter. He opened it and in it was a check for $1,500! Letter and cheek were signed by a laboring man in Massilon, Ohio, who, having heard of the Church's need for an organ, "felt impressed to send the money!"

The second payment came in the same mail with a notice of draft from the organ people for the amount. It was from the executor of an estate in California, saying that the deceased had left the distribution of certain sums to him, and he had decided to send this amount "toward the music in the new Temple!"

The final payment was the most unaccountable of all. Three $100 bills were pushed under the door of the Church study, and a certificate of mining stock worth $700 was sent from Butte, Mont., with nothing on it to indicate from whom it came!

These are just a few instances of answered prayer from the scores of cases mentioned in Conwell's book. Others covered every possible human need, from paying off mortgages to finding lost children, and the safe return without ransom of a kidnapped child!

What is responsible for such results? What is this force released by earnest prayer, that brings about such miraculous results? Can we lay our hands on it, guide it, direct it? Can we depend upon it as a positive, reliable factor, and not a mere whim of fate? Perhaps the following will supply the answer.

Sincerely,
—ROBERT COLLIER

WHAT IS PRAYER?

"But the stars throng out in their glory,
And they sing of the God in man;
They sing of the mighty Master,
Of the loom His fingers span,
Where a star or a soul is part of the whole,
And weft in the wondrous plan."

—ROBERT SERVICE

If you would know the surest way of speeding up your rate of motion, and overtaking the things you desire, try PRAYER!

But when I say "prayer," I don't mean the begging kind. I don't mean a lot of vain repetitions that seldom have the attention even of the one repeating them, much less of the Lord. Go to the Bible, and you will learn how to pray.

Out of 600,000 words in the Old Testament, only six, when literally translated, mean to "ask for" things in prayer, and each of these six is used but once.

Against that, the word "palal" is used hundreds of times to signify "to pray." And "palal" means—"To judge yourself to be a marvel of creation; to recognize amazing wonders deep within your soul."

Wouldn't that seem to indicate that prayer was meant to be a realization of the powers deep within you? Wouldn't you judge that all you need to do is to expand your consciousness to take in whatever it is that you desire?

"What things soever you ask for when you pray, believe that ye receive them, and ye shall have them." You are not to think of your lacks and needs. You are to visualize the things you want! You are not to worry about this debt or that note, but mentally see the Infinite Supply all about you.

9

"All that you need is near ye, God is complete supply. Trust, have faith, then hear ye, dare to assert the 'I'".

Remember this: If you pray to God, but keep your attention on your problem, you will still have your problem. You'll run into it and continue to run into it as long as you keep your attention focused upon it. What you must do is fix your attention upon God—upon His goodness, His love, His power to remedy any ill or adjust any untoward condition. Focus your attention upon these, and these are the conditions you will run into.

Prayer is expansion, and expansion of yourself into the Godself all around you. As Kahlil Gibran describes it in his great book "The Prophet"—"For what is prayer but the expansion of yourself into the living ether. When you pray, you rise to meet in the air those who are praying at that very hour, and whom save in prayer you may not meet. Therefore let your visit to the temple invisible be for naught save ecstasy and sweet communion. I cannot teach you to pray in words. God listens not to your words save when He Himself utters them through your lips."

Prayer is a realization of your Oneness with God, and of the infinite power this gives you. It is an acceptance of the fact that there is nothing on earth you cannot have—once you have mentally accepted the fact that you CAN have it. Nothing you cannot do—once your mind has grasped the fact that you CAN do it.

Prayer, in short, is thanksgiving for the infinite good God has given you. The word most often used for "prayer" in the Old Testament means—"To sing a song of joy and praise."

And how often you see that method used by every great character of the Bible. Running through all their acts and teachings you find the glowing element of praise and thanksgiving.

Go back over the Bible and see how often you are adjured to "Praise the Lord and be thankful, that THEN shall the earth yield her increase." Probably no life chronicled in the

Scriptures was more beset with trials and dangers than that of King David. And what was his remedy? What brought him through all tribulations to power and riches? Just read the Psalms of David and you will see.

"Jehovah reigneth; let the earth rejoice;
Let the multitude of isles be glad.
Bless Jehovah, my soul;
And all that is within me, bless His holy name . . .
Who forgiveth all thine iniquities;
Who healeth all thy diseases."

Throughout the Bible we are told—"In everything by prayer and supplication WITH THANKSGIVING let your requests be made known unto God." Again and again the root of inspiration and attainment is stressed: Rejoice, be glad, praise, give thanks! "Prove me now herewith, saith the Lord of Hosts, if I will not open you the window of Heaven and pour you out a blessing, that there shall not be room enough to receive it."

The most complete interpretation of prayer I have heard came from the man who wrote—"Once I used to say 'Please.' Now I say, 'Thank you.'" "Enter into His gates with thanksgiving," the Psalmist bade us, "and into His courts with praise. Be thankful unto Him and bless His name."

Someone has said that prayer is the spirit of God pronouncing His works good. "This is the day Jehovah hath made. We will rejoice and be glad in it." It is sound psychology as well, as Prof. Wm. James of Harvard testified. "If you miss the joy," he wrote, "you miss all."

Complete, wholehearted reliance upon God—that is the prayer of faith. Not an imploring of God for some specific thing, but a clear, unquestioning recognition that the power to be and do and have the things you want is inherent in you, that you have only to recognize this power and put your trust in it to get anything of good you wish.

But perhaps you have prayed long and fervently for some

particular thing, and it has not come. What then? Has it ever occurred to you that the answer was there, but you didn't receive it because you were not ready or willing to accept it?

God always answers prayer. Over and over He tells us this. The answer to your prayer is as sure as tomorrow's sunrise. YOU are the one who is not sure. You are not sure, and so you do not accept the answer.

If you accepted it, you would act on it, wouldn't you? Did you ever act upon the answer to those long and fervent prayers of yours? Yet that is the way it must be, if you are to pray for an answer—and GET it. If you pray for health, you must accept health. You must act as though you already had it. If you pray for other things, you must accept them at once and start doing—even on the smallest scale—the things you would do when the answer to your prayer became evident.

WAIT THOU ON GOD

My soul, wait thou on God; let thy desire

Be felt so strong that all the holy fire

Aflame upon the altar of my heart

May brand each wish as thine. Let none apart

From thine and God's lead me astray;

I have the good I seek, when thus I pray.

—Anonymous

INNER POWER

I never try to do my work
By my own power alone. When I begin I make my prayer
Before God's holy throne. I ask that His almighty power
May work its will through me,
And so each task is done with ease:
I'm charged with power, you see.

—Hannah Orth

PRAYER WORKS!
By: ROBERT COLLIER

THE easiest way to learn how any principle works is to take it first in its simplest form, see what are the factors that animate it, then follow the working of those factors through all the complicated forms that follow.

So to see how prayer works, let us take the single nerve cell, find the factors that animate it, and then see if these factors do not remain constant even in so complicated an organism as the Mind.

Turn first to the diagram of a typical nerve cell as given in any authoritative medical work. What do you find? From one side of the cell-body a long fibre extends, making connection with some muscle or some part of the skin. This fibre is part of the nerve cell, and carries the stimuli or orders from the cell to the muscle it controls, and it is through it that nervous energy is transformed into muscular energy. Thoughts, emotions, desires, send impulses to the nerve cells, providing the stimuli that set the muscles in action.

So if you have a desire which requires the action of only one muscle, what happens? Your desire takes the form of an impulse to the nerve-cell which controls that muscle; the orders travel along the cell-fibre to the muscle, which promptly contracts in accord with the stimuli given it. And your desire is satisfied.

But suppose the muscle finds the job too great for it alone? Suppose it requires the united power of every muscle in the whole body? As stated above, on one side of each nerve-cell is a long fibre which carries stimuli to the muscle, or else carries messages from the sensory end-plates in the skin to the nerve cell, registering feelings and impressions. But that isn't all! On the other sides are short fibres, apparently ending in space. And as long as the nerves are at rest, these

14

fibres do lie in space.

But stir up the nerve cells, give them a job to do that is greater than the muscles at their command can manage, and then watch these short fibres! They bestir themselves to some purpose. They stir up the nerve-cells near them, and stimulate these in turn to stir up those they contact, until, if necessary, every cell in the whole body is twitching and every muscle tensed ready for any work you may demand.

Now that is what happens when you pray. You are a cell in the great God-body of the Universe. When you work with your hands, your feet, your body, you are using the muscles under the immediate control of your own cell. But that is so infinitesimally small a part of the whole universe. It is as though you tried to do all your work with the tiniest muscle in your little finger, when you could just as well draw upon the power of the entire hand—or, in fact, of the whole body! It is as though some one of your nerve cells thought it had to do the work of the entire body, and tried, with the little muscle at its command, to do that work.

So the wise man does in the God-body, what the wise cell does in your own physical body—he prays! In other words, he stirs up other nerve-cells to use the muscles at their command to help him do the work demanded of him.

And that is all prayer is—using the fibres on the other side of your nerve cell, those fibres that apparently end in space, to stir up all the cells whose action is necessary to the accomplishment of your desire.

That is the reason it was said in the Vedas thousands of years ago that if any two people would unite their psychic forces, they could conquer the world! When two or more nerve cells unite for a certain action, they get that action, even if to bring it about they have to draw upon every cell in the whole body for help!

That does not mean anything is impossible to a single cell or a single person—merely that when two or more are united

15

for a common purpose, the results are easier. But there is no good thing any man can ask, believing, that he cannot get.

In the first chapter of Genesis, it is said that God gave man dominion over the earth. And it is true. It is just as true as that any nerve cell in your whole body has dominion over your body. If you doubt it, let one nerve be sufficiently irritated, and see how quickly it puts every nerve in your body on edge!

One nerve cell in your body, with a strongly held purpose, can bring into action every cell in your body to accomplish that purpose. One nerve cell in the God-body (in other words, one man or woman) with a strongly held purpose, can bring into action every cell in the universe, if these be necessary to the accomplishment of that purpose!

Does that mean anything to you? Does it mean anything to know that the words of prophets and seers are that the promises of the Scriptures can be depended upon, that there really is a Power in the Universe that responds to the urge of the lowliest man or woman just as readily as to the command of the highest?

The world is yours! It matters not whether you be prince or pauper, blue-blooded or red, white-skinned, black, yellow or brown. The God-body of the Universe makes no more distinction between cells than do you in responding to the impulses of the nerve-cells in your own body. Rich or poor—it's all one to you. Highly placed or low—one can cause you as much trouble, or give you as great satisfaction, as another. And the same is true of the God-body of the Universe. The only difference is in understanding and purpose.

How much understanding have you? And what are you doing to increase it? "Seek first understanding, and all things else shall be added unto you." Easier to believe that now, isn't it? With the right understanding, you could run the world! Can you think of anything more important than acquiring understanding?

16

What was it made Napoleon? Certainly not native genius. He came of humble parentage. His brothers were of such ordinary intelligence that throughout his years of power, they were constantly getting him into hot water through their blunders. He himself was backward in his studies. At the Military Academy, he barely managed to pass the tests. He stood forty-sixth in his class—and there were only sixty-five in the class!

Even as a young officer, there was nothing to distinguish him from the thousands of others. He had no inordinate belief in his ability or his destiny—in fact, his letters show him so discouraged over his prospects that he frequently contemplated suicide!

What turned this complaining, discouraged, poverty-stricken and quite ordinary young man into the greatest military genius of his age, "Man of Destiny" and master of most of Europe?

In our own country, we have such outstanding men as Abraham Lincoln, the son of an illiterate pioneer farmer, who learned the little that was taught in the backwoods schools and was employed in rough farm work until the age of 19. Henry Ford, born in modest circumstances on a Michigan farm was educated in district schools. He learned the machinists trade as an apprentice with the Dry Dock Engine Co. and worked in the evenings for a jeweler.

George Washington Carver came of negro slave parents. When he was six weeks old he and his mother were stolen and carried into Arkansas by night riders. George was ransomed for a horse valued at $300; his mother was never seen again. Later he worked his way through school and college. As a scientist he carried on an astonishing series of experiments in developing industrial uses for agricultural products. He was a member of the Royal Society of Arts, London, and received the Spingarn and the Roosevelt medals for his research.

These men were no different from you or me. They had no

more brains or vitality or ability. In their early manhood, they showed no signs of genius. They plodded along like you or me, so much so that no one was more surprised than their old neighbors, who knew them best, when they so suddenly rose to rank and power. As Edgar Guest expressed it in one of his stirring little poems:

"The great were once as you.
They whom men magnify today
Once groped and blundered on life's way,
Were fearful of themselves, and thought
By magic was men's greatness wrought.
They feared to try what they could do;
Yet Fame hath crowned with her success
The selfsame that you possess."

What made the difference? What is there in them that you or I lack? What stirred it into life? What is their Talisman, and where can we find one?

Perhaps the answer is best given in the words of another poet, Berton Braley:

If you want a thing bad enough

To go out and fight for it,

Work day and night for it,

Give up your time and your peace and your sleep for it,

If only desire of it

Makes you quite mad enough

Never to tire of it,

Makes you hold all other things tawdry and cheap for it,

If life seems all empty and useless without it
And all that you scheme and you dream is about it,
If gladly you'll sweat for it,
Fret for it, plan for it,
Lose all your terror of God or man for it,

18

If you'll simply go after that thing that you want,

With all your capacity,
Strength and sagacity,
Faith, hope and confidence, stern pertinacity,
If neither cold poverty, famished and gaunt,
Nor sickness nor pain
Of body or brain
Can turn you away from the thing that you want,
If dogged and grim you besiege and beset it,
YOU'LL GET IT!

In short, the Talisman that stirs the entire body of the Universe into action and brings a whole country or the whole world to your feet, if that be necessary to the accomplishment of your purpose, is the same Talisman as that needed to put the entire physical body at the service of any one nerve cell—a purpose so strongly held that life or death or anything else seems of small consequence beside it! A purpose—and utter faith in it!

Love sometimes makes such a Talisman—the love that goes out to dare all and do all for the loved one. The lust for power is a potent Talisman, that has animated men since time began. Greater still is the zeal of one who would convert the world. That Talisman has carried men through fire and flood, into every danger and over every obstacle; it has changed the face of the world.

Faith in charms, belief in luck, utter confidence in another's leadership, all are Talismans of greater or lesser power.

But the greatest of all is belief in the God inside YOU! Belief in its power to draw to itself every element it needs for expression. Belief in a definite PURPOSE it came here to fulfill, and which can be fulfilled only through YOU!

19

Have you such a faith? If not, get it! Without such a faith, life is purposeless, meaningless. What is more, until you lay hold of that Talisman, life will never bring anything worthwhile to you!

What was it won for Grant over his more brilliant opponents? The grim, dogged, persistent purpose to fight it out along those lines if it took all summer. What is it that has made England victor in so many of her wars, in spite of inept leadership and costly blunders? That same bulldog determination, which holds on in spite of all reverses and discouragements, until its fight is won.

If the nerve in a tooth keeps crying out that a cavity in that tooth needs attention, won't you finally drop everything and seek out a dentist who can satisfy that nerve's needs? And if any other nerve prays continuously for attention, won't you do likewise with it?

Well, you are a nerve in the God-body. If you have an urgent need, and keep praying and insisting and demanding the remedy, don't you suppose you will get it just as surely?

A definite purpose, held to in the face of every discouragement and failure, in spite of all obstacles and opposition, will win no matter what the odds. It is the one nerve cell working against the indifference, the inertia or even the active opposition of the entire group. If the cell is easily discouraged, it will fail. If it is willing to wait indefinitely, it will have to wait. But if it keeps stirring up the cells next to it, and stimulating them to stir those beyond, eventually the entire nerve system will go into action and bring about the result that single cell desires— even if it be only to rid itself of the constant irritation.

You have seen young fellows determined to go to college. You have thought them foolish, in the face of the obstacles facing them. Yet when they persisted, you know how often those obstacles have one by one magically disappeared, until presently they found themselves with the fruition of their desires. A strongly held purpose, persisted in, believed in, is as sure to win in the end as the morrow's sun is to rise. And earnest prayer is to the God-body what a throbbing nerve is to yours. Hold to it, insist upon it, and it is just as sure of a hearing.

A nucleus of whirling energy may gather to itself material elements a hundred or a thousand times as big as itself. But no matter how big it grows, the important part—the activating part—is the nucleus of energy, not the elements it gathers to it.

A comet may have a tail a million times as long as itself. But the tail is merely incidental. The activating principle lies entirely in the comet.

So with you, your life and circumstances. It doesn't matter how much or how little you have, how great your body or how puny—the important thing is the spirit that animates you, the purpose that gives it life.

The famous English scientist, Sir James Jeans, brings out this fact clearly in his book, The Mysterious Universe.

The universe, says Sir James, has no substance. It is nothing but waves, and it exists only in the mind, as an object of thought! "It does not matter," he says, "whether objects exist in the mind or that of any other created spirit or not; their objectivity arises from their subsisting in the mind of some Eternal Spirit.

"Today there is a wide measure of agreement, which on the physical side of science approaches almost to unanimity, that the stream of knowledge is heading toward a non-mechanical reality; the universe begins to look more like a great thought than like a great machine.

"Mind no longer appears as an accidental intruder into the realm of matter; we are beginning to suspect that we ought rather to hail it as the creator and governor of the realm of matter.

"We discover that the universe shows evidence of a

designing or controlling power that has something in common with our own individual minds. And while much of it may be hostile to the material appendages of life, much also is akin to the fundamental activities of life."

In other words, from looking upon life as a mere accident in the primeval slime, from conceiving the universe to be no more than a great machine which somehow got wound up and is now running itself out, from believing man to be merely a higher form of ape, science has progressed until now it sees evidences of the Mind back of all this, it catches glimpses of the Divine plan and marvels at its own temerity in having ever thought to limit that infinite conception.

Mind is the nucleus. All else is merely incidental. And you are part of that great Creative Mind! What does it matter what your circumstances may be, what your surroundings? "They exist only in your mind"—in yours, and the minds of those around you. So why not change them? Why be fettered to an idea, when all you have to do is to realize that there is no substance in it, so disclaim it, discard it and replace it with a better one?

There is no life, power or intelligence in any circumstance or condition. All is Mind, its images and beliefs. Mind forms the molds. Faith fills them. Mind is the Creator. Faith is the builder. Therefore the only things that matter are your mental images and your belief in them.

So what is the remedy for every untoward circumstance and condition? First, to deny it—to take the life of your belief out of it. Destroy your mental image or mold of wrong conditions. Realize that there is no substance in matter—that it is merely so many waves of force, contracted or expanded by thought, so your beliefs are the only things that count. As Sir James Jeans says—"In the scientific process, the old familiar laws of the conservation of matter, of mass and of energy are reduced to one—swallowed up in the law of radiation!"

"In short," one reviewer put it in commenting on his book, "the universe is like a soap bubble, with the insubstantial stars, numbering more than all the sands of all the beaches in the world, floating on its insubstantial surface. Around this empty globe, light curves and bends back on itself, showing that space itself is finite. With an apparently solid earth beneath our feet, the vast framework of heaven above us, and brick and steel to shelter us, it all sounds weird and fantastic, like a feverish dream. But the thought behind it all necessarily implies a Thinker."

You are part of that great Thinker—an independent unit, capable of bringing His entire power to bear upon the solution of your little problems. You are a unit of that Universal Mind, and just as the shoot of the oak tree has every property of the parent oak, just as a drop of water from the ocean has every property of the entire ocean, so have you property of God! You are a creator. You can build your own circumstances and conditions to suit yourself. And if need be, you can call upon the entire body of the universe to help you!

What is it makes the child swim when thrown suddenly into deep water? What was it enabled a paralytic who had not stirred from his bed for five years, to jump out and run up three flights of stairs when the man in the bed next to his suddenly went crazy and tried to lull him? What was it cleared a ward of paralytics, when a ten-foot boa constrictor crawled up the rain pipe and through the window? What was it animated Brown Ladone, bedridden for seventeen years, his knees swollen to the size of water pails, his heart organically diseased—yet when the house caught fire, he not only ran up stairs, but carried down one after another three heavy trunks?

What is it accounts for all the miracles of healing you read about?

1st, the fact that matter is not solid, is not impermeable, is not real substance. If it were, all the excitement in the world, all the emotion, all the faith, could not change it. Matter is FORCE—force manifested in great density, it is true, but none the less force. And when sufficiently stimulated, those waves of force can be made to change their density.

2nd, those waves of force are without intelligence or volition. They respond to impulses in exactly the same way that muscles react to the commands of the nerve cells governing them. And just as your nerve cells can break up any condition of the muscle, so can the nerve cells of the God-Body (of which you are one) break up any condition of your circumstances or surroundings.

Suppose you were paralyzed, unable to move a single muscle, and had been that way for years, as was the case with some of those above-mentioned. Then, in the dead of night, you awoke to the fearsome cry of "Fire!" What would happen? Your central nervous system would call upon every nerve cell in your body to use every muscle at its command to carry you and those dear to you out of danger.

It would not matter if nine-tenths of those cells were paralyzed. As long as there was life in them, the other tenth would put forth such urgent stimulation as to stir up every dormant bit of energy in the nine-tenths and get action out of them. Under the spell of intense emotion, all inhibitions are forgotten and every ounce of energy in the entire nervous system is concentrated on action. There's no time then to think what you can or cannot do; no time for weakness or pain. All the faculties are devoted to the accomplishment of the one purpose, and the sick and the weak and bedridden often show the strength of Hercules!

Why? Because health and strength and intelligence lie not in the muscles or bones or sinews, but in the Mind! And if you can animate the entire nerve organism with one dominating purpose, there is no feat of strength possible to

24

any human body which YOU cannot accomplish. You can break up any condition of your body, reform the waves of force of which you are made in any new mold. All it requires is the intense emotion—and faith.

And in the same way you can break up long-standing conditions in your own body and bring about happier ones, so can you break up wrong conditions in your circumstances and surroundings, and bring about those you desire.

You are a nerve cell in the God-body. That body is made up of waves of force, just as your own is. They respond to the impulses of the nerve cells governing them, just as your muscles do. And those nerve cells can be stimulated into action by other cells, just like those in your own nerve centers.

So get busy stirring them into action! First, take the life out of the conditions you don't want. Disclaim them, let go of them—and forget them! Then image clearly in your mind's eye what you do want, claim it as yours, try to SEE it, FEEL it in your possession, realize that the God-body has no choice but to give it to you if you insist urgently and confidently enough; so believe that you receive! Never doubt it, you'll get it!

That is the answer to "What was the secret of Napoleon?" That is back of every great fortune, every big success. These men demanded their birthright. They believed in their right to success. And instead of cringing and hoping, they reached out for what they wanted and took it!

That is what you too must do. God gave you dominion. He expects you to exercise it. If you don't, it is your loss—not His. He is not going to do your work for you, any more than you do the work for your own nerve cells. When a nerve cell stirs its neighbors into action, it is for its own sake—not theirs. If any nerve cell is too lazy or too inert to work for itself, the others do not bother their heads about it. They go on with their tasks, strengthening their connections with other active cells and the muscles they control until they can do without the lazy one altogether, and if it then passes out of the picture, it is not even missed.

The whole purpose of life is expression. So when you reach out after greater and more comprehensive means of expression, you are working with one of the fundamental laws of the universe, The Law of Tendency. To swim with the tide makes your progress many times safer and easier. All the forces of nature seem to unite to help you on your way.

You want to get ahead, to express life to the fullest degree. How are you to go about it?

First, realize that there is no life in the conditions or circumstances that hedge you around or hold you back now. So disclaim them, and disregard them. Take the life of your belief out of them, and you can shake them off.

Second, set your goal! Decide just what action you do want, just how you can best express life and what is essential to that expression.

Third, use every means at your command to bring about the consummation of your desire, just as the nerve cell first uses the muscle it controls before calling upon other nerve cells for help.

Fourth, PRAY! Pray in the serene knowledge that the great God-body has everything you need for the fruition of your desire. Pray, knowing that yours is the dominion—that if you hold grimly, steadfastly to your purpose, the God-body MUST give you at least some equivalent of your desire.

Lastly, pray, believing—believe that the God-body is acceding to your prayer—believe that you receive! For prayer, as Phillips Brooks reminds us, is not forcing God's reluctance; it is taking hold of God's willingness.

Do that—and there is no good thing you cannot get.

As A. Cressy Morrison says in his splendid book, "Man Does Not Stand Alone": "The richness of religious experience

26

finds the soul of man and lifts him, step by step, until he feels the Divine presence. The instinctive cry of man, "God help me," is natural, and the crudest prayer lifts one closer to his Creator."

"Thou shalt make thy prayer unto Him, and He shall bear thee, and thou shalt pay thy vows. Thou shalt also decree a thing, and it shall be established unto thee; and the light shall shine upon thy ways. When men are cast down, then thou shalt say, there is lifting up; and He shall save the humble person." —Job 22: 27-29.

A PRAYER

Dear Lord, I came to You in prayer,

And I found hope and comfort there. You gave me wisdom, courage, power

That I so needed in that hour.

Before I asked You knew my need;
The answer came with fullest speed.
So graciously with love You fed
My soul the necessary "bread."

Again, dear Lord, come to pray
For guidance, help, along the way.
Teach me things You have me know; Show me the way Your child should go.

Mold me, God, so I may be

Prepared to serve more fittingly;

And in the name of Your dear Son

I ask once more Your will be done.

—BONNIE SOULE REILLY

THE GREATEST DISCOVERY

WHEN the late Dr. Charles Steinmetz, Research Scientist for General Electric Laboratories, was asked in what department of Science the greatest discoveries would be made in the next fifty years, Dr. Steinmetz replied:

"I think the greatest discovery will be made along spiritual lines. Here is a force which history clearly teaches has been the greatest power in the development of man and history. Yet we have been merely playing with it, and have never seriously studied it, as we have the physical forces. Someday people will learn that material things do not bring happiness, and are of little use in making men and women creative and powerful. The scientists of the world will turn their laboratories over to the study of God, PRAYER, and the spiritual forces which have, as yet, hardly been scratched. When this day comes, the world will see more advancement in one generation than it has in the past four."

EFFECTIVE PRAYER
By: RUSSELL H. CONWELL

THE reports of the answers to prayer so often use the words "happened to think" that the observer cannot escape the conviction that either the living human mind does send spirit messages or that some mysterious power acts for it in forwarding messages. The great list of mysterious impulses and intuitions which were noticed in those interesting seasons of prayer could not have been all accidental nor could they be classed under the natural laws of cause and effect. The connection between the cause as seen in the prayer and the effect as related in the "happened-to-think" result is often wholly hidden.

A mother in Philadelphia prayed for her prodigal son and at that exact time the son, alone in a Chicago hotel, felt an uncontrollable influence to turn back to his home. A father prayed that his son might decide to be a missionary, and the son, a sailor off the coast of South America, at that same moment made the decision. A wife prayed that her husband might be sent home sober. At the time she was kneeling by the kitchen table he was waiting at the saloon to be served with brandy, but he "happened to think" that his mother had prayed for him on her deathbed and he could not take the liquor.

A doctor, sadly defeated in his fight for the life of his patient, went to his bedroom and prayed for light, and he "happened to think" that the patient might have swallowed some piece of metal. There was no report of the like symptoms in any case he could find in the medical books. But so deep was the impression that he secured a powerful magnet and drew forth the death-dealing needle. A merchant had an offer for his entire stock which seemed favorable, and, as he was in need, the offer seemed providential. But while the suggestion from the pulpit that each worshiper pray for success in his occupation was being adopted he prayed for his business. At that hour his son in Denver was also praying in church. When he there thought of his father he decided fully to go home and enter business with him. So completely did he decide that the next morning he telegraphed to his surprised and delighted father that he would come home if his father needed his assistance. The joy of having his son at home again overcame his determination to complete a favorable bargain, and he declined the offer promptly. Before the son reached Philadelphia a sudden change in the paper market doubled the sale value of the father's stock.

One writer for a daily newspaper was meditating on some object of prayer in the silence of the praying congregation when the idea of a textbook on journalism for college use came to his mind for the first time. It led directly to a series of syndicate articles which enabled him to purchase the home for which he had been praying. A mechanic who had been out of work, owing to a fire, prayed for a job. At the same time a builder who was a stranger in the church was praying for a competent partner. When the prayers were finished they "happened" to look at each other across the church and each wondered why the other looked at him so intently. The pews in which they sat were at right angles and it was a natural thing for the occupant of one pew to glance at the inmate of the other pew. After church each approached the other with the simultaneous expression, "It seems to me that we have met before." But that was their first meeting. Their firm is now engaged in large construction work in concrete houses and factories. A servant girl in a small home prayed for a dress suitable for church and at that hour her mistress was visiting a friend who remarked that the photograph of a deceased daughter greatly resembled the visitor's servant girl. A few minutes later the friend of the mistress said: "I wonder if my daughter's dresses would fit your servant? If they will fit her, there are here two new gowns that the dressmaker sent home after my daughter's death."

So a young man, without advanced education, prayed hard

for an opportunity to get mental training to fit him for the ministry. At the same moment a principal of a New Jersey academy was in the gallery far removed from the young man and he prayed for direction in finding a suitable janitor. The academy principal mentioned his need to one of the church members who "happened" to know the young man. It was arranged that the young man should work for his board and tuition and have five hours a day for study. The worshiper described himself in his sketch of the answer to his prayers as one whom "God has led into the fulfillment of all his highest ambitions." He is pastor of a strong church, in Cleveland.

A little tot prayed for a "singing doll," and her mother told her that a doll was too small a matter to pray for. But the father overheard the conversation, and, after purchasing the most costly one he could find at his noon hour, he left it on the little one's bed in the night when everyone else was supposed to be asleep. A widow prayed for some leadership in the sale of some wild land in Louisiana. Her relatives urged her to let it go, as the "taxes will soon eat it all." But the unexpected payment of a debt due her led her to feel that, as she had been temporarily provided for, she would wait. In about seven weeks she read in a paper that a company had struck oil on the next section to her estate. She consequently leased the mineral privileges of her land at a high price.

A student whose mental faculties were unusually dull for his age prayed that he might pass his examination in mathematics. That night in his dreams his subconscious self worked out plainly on a blackboard the two hardest problems. A farmer prayed for some deciding hint in his choice of seed for his land. On his way home he held a bundle in his lap which was in a newspaper wrapper. In one column on the wrapper directly under his eyes was an article on the soils and products of his country which opened his vision and made his farming safe and profitable. An Alsatian girl prayed that her father and mother might come to America. They knew nothing of her petition, but on

32

that same day and hour, allowing for the difference in the reckoning of time, the parents resolved to come to America, and financial aid was promised them.

A lawyer was asking the Lord for some clue to lost evidence, so necessary to his case to be tried the next day, when the name of a witness whose relation to the case he had not before thought of, and whose name had been long forgotten, was suggested to him. While doubtful of the value of the witness, he sought his name in the directory and found that the lost witness was all-sufficient for the case. A dealer in real estate asked the Lord to prosper a proposed transaction, if it were for the best, and to hinder it if it would be injurious. He unintentionally omitted the word "not" from the draft of a contract which he drew the next day and the "accidental" omission brought him to unexpected possession of a profitable block of houses.

To the unbeliever all these testimonals prove but little. But to the experienced observer of repeated answers to prayer they are conclusive proofs of God's disposition to answer the "effectual, fervent prayer of the righteous man." As a woman may feel when she puts her weary life into the care of a strong and affectionate husband, the trusting believer in prayer rests in God in a peaceful condition of soul, which passeth all understanding.

THE PRAYER OF FAITH

"God is my help in every need;
God does my every hunger feed;
God walks beside me, guides my way
Through every moment of the day.

I now am wise, I now am true,
Patient, kind and loving, too.
All things I am, can do and be,
Through God, the Truth, that is in me.

God is my health; I am well and strong;
God is my joy, the whole day long;
God is my All, I know no fear,
Since God and Love and Truth are here."

—HANNAH MOORE KOHAUS

WANTED: LEADERS
By: ROBERT COLLIER

A GOOD many years ago, Professor Henry of Princeton made an experiment with a charged magnet.

First he took an ordinary magnet of large size, suspended it from a rafter, and with it lifted a few pounds of iron.

Then he wrapped the magnet with wire and charged it with the current from a small battery. Instead of only a few pounds, the now highly charged magnet lifted 3,000 pounds!

That is what happens when one person prays and believes, and another adds his faith in the efficacy of that prayer. The second person is the battery. His faith is the current, which multiplies the power of the other's prayer a dozen times over.

There are people with such great faith that they can pray, and get unfailing results through their own efforts alone.

But most of us can hope for the best results only when, like Professor Henry, we charge our magnet with the current from an outside battery.

I have known exponents of the mental sciences to treat children without the knowledge of their parents. And frequently the treatments failed. Yet when later those same practitioners worked upon the children with the active faith of a parent or others to help, the treatments were successful!

Why? Because when working alone, they had nothing to give but the power latent in their own minds, whereas with the faith of others to help, they were like Professor Henry's charged magnet.

You see, helping others is not a mere matter of cheering them, or advising them, or showing them how to help themselves. You must actually GIVE something of yourself to them, some of your vital forces, some of your magnetism.

The great cry of today is for Leaders—men and women who can lift their fellows out of the slough of des-pond, who can show them how to unite their prayers or their forces to get what they want! And what is the secret of such leading? Neither more nor less than the secret Prof. Henry discovered—getting a group to unite in GIVING their current to strengthen the magnet of some one of their number, that thus he may draw to him what he needs. That is all religion is—a binding together for a common purpose. The word religion is derived from the Latin re and ligo, meaning—" to bind together.

How about YOU? Have you the urge to be such a Leader? I don't mean—are you trained for it? Training and instruction can follow. The Apostles were common men, for the most part uneducated men, with no experience in leadership. But they had the urge, and the means to satisfy that urge quickly followed.

Phillip Brooks once said—"We feel the thing we ought to be, beating beneath the thing we are." That is the urge which carries those who heed it on to greatness. Have you it?

If you have, then put it to work! Start now—this minute— using it. The only way to get training is through practice. The only way to become a Leader is to start leading, even though you have in the beginning only one or two to follow. The line will grow.

And remember this: There is no surer way of winning riches or health or happiness for yourself than by bringing these into the lives of those around you. As in the case of Job —"The Lord turned the captivity of Job, when he prayed for his friends."

"For who upon the hearth can start a fire,
And never warm the stone?
Or who can cheer another's heart,

36

And not his own? "I stilled a hungry infant's cry,
With kindness filled a stranger's cup,
And lifting others, found that I
Was lifted up!"

Plato tells us of a race of winged men who conquered all others through their ability to rise above every obstacle, to surmount every difficulty.

Today we have, in the airplane, the physical wings to carry us far above the clouds, but still we lag behind many ancient philosophers in acquiring the mental wings to lift us over the bogs of sickness and the tangled wilderness of want.

Yet a few have acquired them. And more are growing them. But it needs leaders to show the way. Will YOU be one? You CAN, you know. Anyone who has intelligently followed us thus far is qualified to help others on their way.

It doesn't matter whether you or your friends think you worthy to do such work. You can brush such objections aside, because it is not YOU that is going to do it. It is "the Father working through you." You are just a willing and intelligent tool in the hands of the Master Craftsman, and "His grace is sufficient for you."

You see, it is not as though you had to do anything to those you want to help, whether their affliction be in their bodies or their homes or their business. You don't have to heal them. The one you need to work upon is yourself!

It is as though their bodies, their circumstances and surroundings were part of a great bas-relief, like the images of the Confederate Generals on Stone Mountain. If their images seem to you to be imperfect, if they are lacking in necessaries of body or surroundings, your first duty to them is to deny that lack. Say aloud—"That is not theirs. That is no part of their perfect image. God's image of them is perfect and complete. This apparent lack or imperfection is merely a mist come between that image and me."

Pause for a moment and try to see in your mind's eye God's

perfect image of them and their surroundings, then GIVE of your magnetic current to help MANIFEST that complete image. Charge the Seed of God in you to use its power to brush away the mist that hides their real image from you. Direct that Seed of Life to give of its power as much as is necessary to draw to them all the elements they need to make their perfect image manifest. And finally, BELIEVE THAT YOU RECEIVE!

Of course, you cannot help anyone against his will, any more than you can hypnotize another without his consent. To get the best results, there must be cooperation, belief. Without another's belief to help you, you are like Prof. Henry's magnet and no battery.

So ask the one you are trying to help to put himself in a receptive mood. Bid him relax utterly, mentally and physically. Explain to him that he doesn't have to DO anything—just LET the water of life soak in. All you require of him is that he sit back in serene faith, neither questioning nor resisting anything you may say, but tearing down all the inhibitions with which he has walled himself around, and LETTING your words and your thoughts penetrate unquestioned to his subconscious self.

Start by realizing that whatever his trouble may be, it does not belong to him. He is a thought in God's Mind, and as such, he is perfect. So disclaim the seeming imperfection or lack. Brush it aside as none of his. Then claim God's perfect idea of him. Know that it is as perfect now as when first God imaged him. Affirm aloud that he is building the physical correspondence of that perfect thought of God's. Affirm it—KNOW THAT HE HAS IT—and mentally give of your own force to help manifest it in him.

The whole purpose of life here on earth is to express God. Every kind act, every good deed, is expressing Him. Every business that faithfully serves mankind expresses Him. Everything you do to make this world more livable expresses Him. So how can you serve Him better than by helping those you know, to live in comfort and happiness and health? And helping them, you could not if you would, avoid being yourself made comfortable, happy and healthy. As Barrie says—"Those who bring happiness into the lives of others, cannot keep it from themselves."

But why should it be necessary for you to give of your magnetic current to help others? Because there must always be someone to release power, someone with the understanding and the faith to say—"Let this thing come to pass!"

People lack the faith to USE the life in themselves. With unlimited energy at their own command, they put their faith in things outside themselves—in drugs, or doctors, or people like you who will do their mental work for them. They want something or someone to lean upon. And that is the whole basis of successful healing, in medicine or in metaphysics—to give the patient something outside himself in which he has greater faith to cure him, than in the power of the disease to do him harm.

You can be a practitioner. There is as much of God in you as in any man or woman in the universe. Not only that, but there is as much of God in you as in any man or woman who ever lived!

You do not need to leave your own Church. You do not need to change your faith. You need only to believe in the perfection and the unchangeableness of God's images.

You remember the old story of the farmer who went to a circus and for the first time gazed upon a giraffe. He looked it over incredulously for a minute, then turned away disgustedly—"There ain't no such animal!" he said.

When you go to the circus of human beliefs, when God's children come to you contorted into all manner of miserable shapes, don't be afraid to say, like the old farmer—"There ain't no such animal !"

39

God has no such thoughts of His children. "For I know the thoughts that I think toward you, saith the Lord. Thoughts of peace, and not of evil."

So when you are called upon to help those in misery or pain, don't hesitate to disclaim those conditions. God has no such images. They are not His. Therefore they cannot be real. Brush away the mists that contort them into such ridiculous images, and LET HIS PERFECT THOUGHT SHOW THROUGH!

In his Teaching and Addresses, Edward A. Kimball puts the whole idea of mental healing into a couple of paragraphs so clearly that I quote them here:

"Suppose you have to treat an insane woman who believes she is covered with feathers. She says she has them. Would you treat her for the purpose of removing feathers? Are there any to deal with? Or would you know that you must abolish such a belief? Now then, suppose your patient says that his lungs are half gone. Do you work any more in the realm of decayed lungs than in the realm of feathers? Do you have such a bodily condition to deal with or have you just to abolish the mesmerism of belief in such a condition? Watch yourself. See that your treatments are not treatments for feathers.

"Knowing Truth is treatment. Only the likeness of God is man. Treatments are failures because we think we have a sick man or woman to treat. That is only a belief in mortal mind law. Do not treat fever any more than you would feathers in an insane woman. No pain, no claim of pain, only the action of mortal mind. Do not annihilate, but displace error with right ideas. The true idea is always the Saviour."

In short, all mental healing comes down to this—that your body is the mirror of your thoughts.

You look in an ordinary mirror, and what do you see there? A reflection—a perfect reflection of your body. Grimace with pain, and your reflection will grimace likewise. Double up your legs, and your reflection will follow suit. Smile, look happy—and your reflection will be as happy as you.

Your body is just as truly a reflector of your innermost beliefs as the mirror on the wall. Believe you have been exposed to contagion, and your body will promptly reflect the symptoms. Believe you are growing old, and your body will begin to reflect the signs of age.

What is the treatment? As Kimball says, don't try to annihilate sickness. Displace it! If your image in the mirror showed a frowning face, you wouldn't try to rub off the frown. You would displace it with a smile. You don't have to fight sickness. All you need to do is to displace it with the healthy image—and the sickness vanishes of itself.

Remember this: When you treat a sickness, it is just as though you worked over your frown in an effort to improve it. You are working on conditions—not causes. If you want real results, go back to the primary cause, which is in God's thought of your patient is of a perfect body. Get hold of that thought—AND KEEP HOLD OF IT! Then put your life, all your belief, into that thought. When it displaces YOUR belief in your patient's illness, his body will mirror your perfect thought of him. When a thing no longer disturbs you, you are through with it.

That is all there is to mental healing. You don't treat a headache, or a rheumatic joint or an ulcer. You blandly wipe them off the picture, and ask yourself—"What is God's thought of this organ?" Your only treatment, if it can be called such, is in putting your light and life into God's perfect picture of the organ the patient thinks diseased, in remembering that He has but one mold of that organ. All others are manmade. Disregard these manmade pictures. Disclaim them. And claim God's perfect image. Claim it—and put your faith and your life into developing that picture.

That is the Alpha and the Omega of mental healing. That is all any practitioner can do. That is what we expect YOU to do—bring together a group of your friends, or of those in need of help, AND LEAD THEM!

PRAYER

... MORE things are wrought by prayer
Than this world dreams of. Wherefore, let thy voice
Rise like a fountain for me night and day.
For what are men better than sheep or goats
That nourish a blind life within the brain,
If, knowing God, they lift not hands of prayer
Both for themselves and those who call them friend?
For so the whole round earth is every way
Bound by gold chains about the feet of God."

—ALFRED, LORD TENNYSON

THE PRAYER CIRCLE
By: REV. W. H. LEATHEN

LIEUTENANT ROGER FENTON had a lump his throat when he said good-bye to his boys. There they were in a bunch on the station platform, the ten wayward lads into whom he had sought to instill the fear of God on Tuesday evenings in winter, and with whom he had rambled and played cricket every Saturday afternoon in summer. Boys of fourteen to seventeen are a tough proposition, and though would answer for their bowling and batting he wasn't over sanguine about their religion. But they had filled a big place in his lonely life in the dull little country town, and now he had to leave them and lose them. For the great call had reached him, and he bore the King's commission, and in his heart was the feeling that he would never come back.

Now the chaff and the parting words of good luck were over, and the train was panting to be off. "Boys," he cried suddenly, "I want you to do something for me, something hard." "Anything you like, sir," they answered eagerly. But their faces fell when they heard their teacher's word. "Look here," he said, "it's this. You'll meet in the old place every Tuesday evening for a few minutes and pray for me that I may do my duty, and, if it please God, that I may come back to you all. And I'll pray for you at the same time even if I'm in the thick of battle."

I wish you had seen the dismay on those ten faces. It was any odds on their blurting out a shamefaced refusal, but Ted Harper, their acknowledged chief, pulled himself together just in time, and called out as the train began to move:"We'll do it, sir. I don't know how we'll manage it, but we'll do our best. "We'll not go back on you."

As Fenton sank into his corner he was aware of the mocking looks of his brother officers. "I say," said one of them, "you don't really think those chaps are going to hold a prayer meeting for you every week, and if they did you can't believe it would stop an enemy's bullet or turn an enemy's shell. It's all very well to be pious, but that's a bit too thick."

Fenton flushed, but he took it in good part. "Prayer's a big bit of our religion," he said, "and I've a notion these prayers will help me. Anyhow I'm sure my lads will do their part. Where Ted Harper leads, they follow."

And sure enough the boys did their part. It was fine to see them starting out in the wrong direction, and twisting and doubling through the crooked lanes till they worked round to the Mission Hall, and then in with a rush and a scuttle, that as few as possible might see. The doings of the crowd, as they were known locally, were the talk of the town in those first days after Roger departed. Would they meet? Would they keep it up? Would they bear the ridicule of the other boys of their own age? And how in the world would they pray?

Time answered all these questions except the last. They met, they continued to meet, they faced ridicule like heroes. But how did they pray? That mystery was as deep and insoluble as before, for whatever awful oath of secrecy bound them to silence not a whisper of the doings of those Tuesday evenings was divulged to the outside world.

I was the only one who ever knew, and I found out by chance. Ted Harper had borrowed "Fights for the Flag" from me, and when I got it back there was a soiled piece of paper in it with something written in Ted's ungainly hand. I thought he had been copying a passage, and anxious to see what had struck him, I opened the sheet out and read these words:-"O God, it's a hard business praying. But Roger made me promise. And you know how decent he's been to me and the crowd. Listen to us now, and excuse the wrong words, and bring him back safe. And, God, make him the bravest soldier that ever was, and give him the V. C. That's what we all want for him. And don't let the war be long, for God's sake. Amen."

I felt a good deal ashamed of myself when I came to the end of this artless prayer. I had got their secret. I could see them kneeling round the Mission forms, two or three with crumpled papers in their hands. They were unutterably shy of religious expression, and to read was their only chance. The boys on whom the fatal lot fell the previous Tuesday were bound to appear with their written devotions a week later.

This war has given us back the supernatural, but no miracle seems more wonderful to me than those ten lads and their ill-written prayers. And, remember, that liturgical service lasted six months, and never a break in the Tuesday meeting. What a grand thing a boy's heart is, when you capture its loyalty and its affection.

It was a black day when the news came. The local Territorials had advanced too far on the wing of a great offensive, and had been almost annihilated. The few survivors had dug themselves in, and held on till that bitter Tuesday faded into darkness and night. When relief came, one man was left alive. He was wounded in four places, but he was still loading and firing, and he wept when they picked him up and carried him away to first aid. That solitary hero, absolutely the only survivor of our local regiment, was Lieutenant Roger Fenton, V.C.

When his wounds were healed, and the King had done the needful bit of decoration, we got him home. We did not make the fuss they did in some places. Our disaster was too awful, and the pathos of that solitary survivor too piercing. But some of us were at the station, and there in the front row were the ten men of prayer. Poor Roger quite broke down when he saw them. And he could find no words to thank them. But he wrung their hands till they winced with the pain of that iron grip.

That night I got a chance of a talk with him alone. He was too modest to tell me anything of his own great exploit. But there was evidently something he wanted to say, and it was as if he did not know how to begin. At last he said, "I have a story to tell that not one in fifty would listen to. That Tuesday evening when I was left alone, and had given up all hope, I remembered it was the hour of the old meeting, and I kept my promise and prayed for the boys of my Class. Then everything around me faded from my mind, and I saw the dear lads in the Mission Room at prayer. I don't mean that I went back in memory. I knew with an absolute certainty that I was there invisible in that night's meeting. Whether in the body or out of the body, I cannot say, but there I was, watching and listening."

"How wonderful!" I said.

"That's not all, there's something stranger still," he went on. "They were kneeling on the floor, and Ted Harper was reading a prayer, and when it was done they said 'Amen' as with one voice. I counted to see if they were all there. I got to ten right enough, but I did not stop there. I counted again, and this is the odd thing—here were elevenof them! In my dream or vision or trance, call it what you will, I was vaguely troubled by this unexpected number. I saw the ten troop out in their old familiar way, and I turned back to find the eleventh, The Comrade in White, and to speak to Him. I felt His presence still, and was glad of it, for the trouble and perplexity were all gone and in their place a great expectation. I seemed to know the very place where He had been kneeling, and I hurried forward. But there was nothing to be seen, nothing but the well-remembered text staring down at me from the wall—'For where two or three are gathered together in my name, there am I in the midst of them.' I remembered no more, till I found myself in the base hospital. But of course I knew then how I had been saved, and what my boys had done for me.

"It makes a man feel strange to have his life given back to him like that; it's as if God would expect a great deal in return. But there's a stronger feeling still in my heart. I believe the lads got their answer not for my sake but for their own. Think what it means to them. They've got their feet now on the rock of prayer. They know the truth of God.

I'm not sure, but I don't think I'll ever tell them that I saw God in their midst. They know it in their own way, and perhaps their own way is best."

He shall call upon me, and I will answer him: I will be with him in trouble; I will deliver him, and honour him.

—Ps. 91:15.

MY PRAYER

GOD, let me live each lovely day
So I may know that, come what may,
I've done my best to live the way
You want me to.

Forgive me if I do not pray
The ultra-sanctimonious way
In church on every Sabbath day
As some folks do.

Just let me know, if I should stray
That I may stop along the way

At any time of night or day—

And talk to you!

—Elsie Janis

HOW TO PRAY
By: R. A. TORREY

IF we would know the fullness of blessing that there is in the prayer life, it is important not only that we pray in the right way, but also that we pray at the right time. Our sages' own examples are full of suggestiveness as to the right time for prayer.

Many of the mightiest men of God have chosen the early morning hour for prayer. In the morning hour the mind is fresh and at its very best. It is free from distraction, and that absolute concentration upon God which is essential to the most effective prayer is most easily possible in the early morning hours. Furthermore, when the early hours are spent in prayer the whole day is sanctified, and power is obtained for overcoming its temptations, and for performing its duties. More can be accomplished in prayer in the first hours of the day than at any other time during the day. Every child of God who would make the most out of his life, should set apart the first part of the day to meeting God in the study of His Word and in prayer. The first thing we do each day should be to go alone with God and face the duties, the temptations, and the service of that day, and get strength from God for all. We should get victory before the hour of trial, temptation or service comes. The secret place of prayer is the place to fight our battles and gain our victories. Our forefathers prayed before all the great crises in their life.

Whenever any crisis of life is seen to be approaching, we should prepare for it by a season of very definite prayer to God. We should take plenty of time for this prayer. The great men of the Bible prayed not only before the great events and victories of their lives, but they also prayed after its great achievements and important crises.

It is more common for most of us to pray before the great

49

events of life than it is to pray after them, but the latter is as important as the former. If we would pray after the great achievements of life, we might go on to still greater; as it is we are often either puffed up or exhausted by the things that we do in the name of the Lord, and so we advance no further. Many and many a man in answer to prayer has been endued with power and thus has wrought great things in the name of the Lord, and when these great things were accomplished, instead of going alone with God and humbling himself before Him, and giving Him all the glory for what was achieved, he has congratulated himself upon what has been accomplished, has become puffed up. The great things done were not followed by humiliation of self, and prayer to God, and so pride has come in and the mighty man has been shorn of his power.

Some men are so busy that they find no time for prayer. Other men of God, once mighty, have lost their power because they did not learn this secret, and allowed increasing work to crowd out prayer.

Years ago it was the writer's privilege, with other theological students, to ask questions of one of the most useful Christian men of the day. The writer was led to ask,

"Will you tell us something of your prayer life?"

The man was silent a moment, and then, turning his eyes earnestly upon me, replied:

"Well, I must admit that I have been so crowded with work of late that I have not given the time I should to prayer."

Is it any wonder that that man lost power, and the great work that he was doing was curtailed in a very marked degree? Let us never forget that the more the work presses on us, the more time must we spend in prayer.

Many temptations come upon us unawares and unannounced, and all that we can do is to lift a cry to God for help then and there; but many of the temptations of life we can see approaching from the distance, and in such cases the victory should be won before the temptation really

50

reaches us.

Our whole life should be a life of prayer. We should walk in constant communion with God. There should be a constant upward looking of the soul to God. We should walk so habitually in His presence that even when we awake in the night it would be the most natural thing in the world for us to speak to Him in thanksgiving or in petition.

In approaching God to ask for new blessings, we should never forget to return thanks for blessings already granted. If any one of us would stop and think how many of the prayers which we have offered to God have been answered, and how seldom we have gone back to God to return thanks for the answers thus given, I am sure we would be overwhelmed with confusion. We should be just as definite in returning thanks as we are in prayer. We come to God with most specific petitions, but when we return thanks to Him, our thanksgiving is indefinite and general.

Doubtless one reason why so many of our prayers lack power is because we have neglected to return thanks for blessings already received. If anyone were to constantly come to us asking help from us, and should never say "Thank you" for the help thus given, we would soon tire of helping one so ungrateful. Indeed, regard for the one we were helping would hold us back from encouraging such rank ingratitude.

Returning thanks for blessings already received increases our faith and enables us to approach God with new boldness and new assurance. Doubtless the reason so many have so little faith when they pray is because they take so little time to meditate upon and thank God for blessings already received. As one meditates upon the answers to prayers already granted, faith waxes bolder and bolder, and we come to feel in the very depths of our souls that there is nothing too hard for the Lord. As we reflect upon the wondrous goodness of God toward us on the one hand, and

51

on the other hand upon the little thought and strength and time that we ever put into thanksgiving, we may well humble ourselves before God.

The mighty men of prayer in the Bible, and the mighty men of prayer throughout the ages have been men who were much given to thanksgiving and praise. David was a mighty man of prayer, and how his Psalms abound with thanksgiving and praise. The apostles were mighty men of prayer; of them we read that "they were continually in the temple, praising and blessing God."

Thanksgiving is one of the inevitable results of being filled with the Holy Spirit and one who does not learn "in everything to give thanks" cannot continue to pray in the Spirit. If we would learn to pray with power we would do well to let these two words sink deep into our hearts: "WITH THANKSGIVING."

Oftentimes when we come to God in prayer, we do not feel like praying. What shall one do in such a case? Cease praying until he does feel like it? Not at all. When we feel least like praying is the time when we most need to pray. We should wait quietly before God and tell Him how cold and prayerless our hearts are, and look up to Him and trust Him and expect Him to send the Holy Spirit to warm our hearts and draw them out in prayer. It will not be long before the glow of the Spirit's presence will fill our hearts, and we will begin to pray with freedom, directness, earnestness, and power. Many of the most blessed seasons of prayer I have ever known have begun with a feeling of utter deadness and prayerlessness; but in my helplessness and coldness I have cast myself upon God, and looked to Him to send His Holy Spirit to teach me to pray, and He has done it.

When we pray in the Spirit, we will pray for the right things and in the right way. There will be joy and power in our prayer.

God does not always let us get things at our first effort. He would train us and make us strong men by compelling us to work hard for the best things. So also He does not always give us what we ask in answer to the first prayer; He would train us and make us strong men of prayer by compelling us to pray hard for the best things. He makes us pray through.

I am glad that this is so. There is no more blessed training in prayer than that that comes through being compelled to ask again and again and again even through a long period of years before one obtains that which he seeks from God. Many people call it submission to the will of God when God does not grant them their requests at the first or second asking, and they say:

"Well, perhaps it is not God's will."

As a rule this is not submission, but spiritual laziness. We do not call it submission to the will of God when we give up after one or two efforts to obtain things by action; we call it lack of strength of character. When the strong man of action starts out to accomplish a thing, if he does not accomplish it the first or second or one hundredth time, he keeps hammering away until he does accomplish it; and the strong man of prayer when he starts to pray for a thing keeps on praying until he prays it through, and obtains what he seeks. We should be careful about what we ask from God, but when we do begin to pray for a thing we should never give up praying for it until we get it, or until God makes it very clear and very definite to us that it is not His will to give it.

One of the great needs of the present day is men and women who will not only start out to pray for things, but pray on and on and on until they obtain that which they seek from the Lord.

AN ENGLISH CHILD PRAYS

I was in my church and a little boy walked in and was soon lost in prayer. He remained on his knees, and I marveled at him. As he went out I asked him if he often came here. To which he replied, "Five times in the last six days." I asked if he had some relations fighting at Dunkerque. He replied, "Yes, my daddy; but he came home this morning, and so I just came in here to thank God."

—The Rector of Woolwich.

I BELIEVE IN PRAYER
By: EDDIE RICKENBACKER

THERE are a lot of things about the human mind and soul that we don't know much about. We get glimpses of them when in times of danger or suffering we cross a little way over the line of ordinary thought.

As I roared down the last stretch in an automobile race years ago, I felt that I could control that machine with my mind, that I could hold it together with my mind, and that if it finally collapsed I could run it with my mind. It was a feeling of mastery, of supreme confidence. But it was real.

If I had said such a thing then, the boys would have called me crazy. Even now I can't explain it. But I believe that if you think disaster you will get it. Brood about death, and you hasten your demise. Think positively and masterfully, with confidence and faith, and life becomes more secure, more fraught with action, richer in achievement and experience.

Perhaps such things as the control of mind over matter and the transmission of thought waves are tied up together, part of something so big we haven't grasped it yet. It's part of us and part of the Something that is looking after us. It's one of the things that make me believe in personal protection and in life after death. I don't know how to put it into words.

Another strange thing happened to me. Several years ago I was flying to Chicago. It was a Sunday afternoon in the middle of December and the weather was miserable. There was a lot of ice. We suddenly lost the radio beam. For a long time we cruised back and forth trying to pick it up. Fog was all around us. We were lost, off the beam, and flying blind. Our two-way radio went out, and we had lost all communication with the world. For seven hours we flew— where, we didn't know. Nobody knew where we were; nobody even knew we were lost.

Darkness was coming on. Then suddenly, we saw a break in the murk. The pilot brought the ship down to within one hundred feet, and we saw lights go flashing by on a four-lane highway.

"It must be going from some place to some place," I said, and we followed it for some distance.

Then we saw a red glow away off to the right, headed for it, and saw a river gleaming. We flew up that river, and out of the six-thirty dusk of winter sprang a town—Toledo! I saw the Toledo-Edison sign flashing as we swept over the bridge tops. Slumming the roofs, we circled and landed at the airport a moment later. We had just enough gas left for eleven minutes of flight.

We had flown blind, without a beam, but we were on a beam, just the same. I like to think it was the "Big Radio" that kept us going—the thing that keeps all of us flying safely through the fog and night, toward some mysterious and important goal. The "Big Radio" is a two-way job.

You've got to keep tuned with It, and you have to talk back. I believe in prayer. I learned to pray as a kid at my mother's knee.

One day in France, with only one magneto on my Nieuport biplane functioning, I was attacked by three German Albatross planes. I came out of a dive so fast that the terrific pressure collapsed my righthand upper wing. No matter what I tried I couldn't come out of that whirl of death. I often wish I could think as fast under normal conditions as I did during that drop. While I fought the controls and tried to get the engine going, I saw all the good and bad things I had ever done, and most of them were bad. Then I began to pray.

"Oh, God," I said, "help me get out of this."

As a last desperate act, I threw my weight to the lefthand side over the cockpit and jammed the controls, then jammed the engine wide open. The thing suddenly sputtered and vibrated violently, and sailed away on her one

56

good wing for France. I held it that way all the way home.

This escape and others I have had were not the result of any super-ability or super-knowledge on my part. I wouldn't be alive if I had to depend on that. I realized then, as I headed for France on one wing, that there had to be Something Else. I had seen others die—brighter and more able than I. I knew there was a Power. I believe in calling upon It for help.

I am not such an egoist as to believe that God has spared me because I am I. I believe there is work for me to do, and I am spared to do it, just as you are. If I die tomorrow I do not fear the prospect at all.

On a rainy night in February, 1941, I had the worst accident of my life. As I look back on those agonizing days in the hospital, I realize there was a reason behind it all. It was a test and a preparation for what was to follow.

In the four months I lay in that hospital I did more thinking about life and death than I had ever done before. Twenty-one months later, I was adrift in an open lifeboat with seven other starving men, most of them so young they needed the strength and understanding of a man who had been down in the valley of the shadow, who had suffered and made sense out of his suffering. To those men I was able to bring the essence of the religion and philosophy I had distilled in the hospital.

Once I almost died from a throat hemorrhage. "Here," I said, "is death." It dawned upon me in a flash that the easiest thing in the world is to die; the hardest is to live. Dying was a sensuous pleasure; living was a grim task. In that moment I chose to live. I knew from experience that abandonment to death was a sin. I was quitting. I had work to do, others to serve.

Many things came to me. I realized I wasn't afraid to die, because I have lived so much in good ways and bad that I no longer feel the youthful pang of not having lived at all. I knew only the sorrow of being unable any more to help

57

other people. And when I finally came around I saw life and death and the meaning of the Golden Rule more clearly than I had ever known.

I took that clarity with me to the rubber raft in the South Pacific after our plane crashed. I shall not recount that story again. I merely want to tell you the meaning of it. Of the eight men in those three rafts, I alone never lost faith that we would be picked up. Throughout those twenty-one days of blistering sun and nights of ghastly chill, we were adrift for a purpose. I saw life had no meaning except in terms of helping others.

I humbly think man instinctively does not interest himself in others. He does it by an act of will. He sees that "my brother's keeper" and "Do unto others" are the essence of all truth.

My experiences and the suffering through which I passed taught me that faith in God is the answer to life.

Recently, in a rehabilitation hospital, I addressed a group of disabled veterans. Many were discouraged; the future looked dark and unpromising. I knew how they felt...I too had been through a lot, but had found a secret which brought me through, and I urged them to find the same secret.

I said, "If you have not had an experience of God in your life, my advice is to get busy and get yourself one." For that is the sure way to win victories over inner defeat. It is the way a humble man meets life or death.

In the day of my trouble I will call upon thee: for thou wilt answer me.

—Ps. 86:7.

PRAYER IS POWER
By: ALEXIS CARREL, M.D.

PRAYER is not only worship; it is also an invisible emanation of man's worshiping spirit—the most powerful form of energy that one can generate. The influence of prayer on the human mind and body is as demonstrable as that of secreting glands. Its results can be measured in terms of increased physical buoyancy, greater intellectual vigor, moral stamina, and a deeper understanding of the realities underlying human relationships.

If you make a habit of sincere prayer, your life will be very noticeably and profoundly altered. Prayer stamps with its indelible mark our actions and demeanor. A tranquility of bearing, a facial and bodily repose are observed in those whose inner lives are thus enriched. Within the depths of consciousness a flame kindles, and man sees himself. He discovers his selfishness, his silly pride, his fears, his greeds, his blunders. He develops a sense of moral obligations, intellectual humility. Thus begins a journey of the soul toward the realm of grace.

Prayer is a force as real as terrestrial gravity. As a physician, I have seen men, after all other therapy had failed, lifted out of disease and melancholy by the serene effort of prayer. It is the only power in the world that seems to overcome the so-called "laws of nature"; the occasions on which prayer has dramatically done this have been termed "miracles." But constant, quieter miracles takes place hourly in the hearts of men and women who nave discovered that prayer supplies them with a steady now of sustaining power in their daily lives.

Too many people regard prayer as a formalized routine of words, a refuge for weaklings, or a childish petition for material things. We sadly undervalue prayer when we conceive it in these terms, just as we should underestimate rain by describing it as something that fills the birdbath in our garden. Properly understood, prayer is a mature activity indispensable to the fullest development of personality—the ultimate integration of man's highest faculties. Only in prayer do we achieve that complete and harmonious assembly of body, mind and spirit which gives the frail human reed its unshakable strength.

Prayer, like radium, is a source of luminous, self-generating energy.

How does prayer fortify us with so much dynamic power? To answer this question (admittedly outside the jurisdiction of science) I must point out that all prayers have one thing in common. The triumphant hosannas of a great oratorio, or the humble supplication of an Iroquois hunter begging for luck in the chase, demonstrate the same truth; that human beings seek to augment their finite energy by addressing themselves to the infinite source of all energy. When we pray, we link ourselves with the inexhaustible motive power that spins the universe. We ask that a part of this power be apportioned to our needs. Even in asking, our human deficiencies are filled and we arise strengthened and repaired.

But we must never summon God merely for the gratification of our whims. We derive most power from prayer when we use it, not as a petition, but as a supplication that we may become more like Him. Prayer should be regarded as practice of the Presence of God. An old peasant was seated alone in the last pew of the village church. "What are you waiting for?" he was asked; and he answered, "I am looking at Him and He is looking at me." Man prays not only that God should remember him, but also that he should remember God.

How can prayer be defined? Prayer is the effort of man to reach God, to commune with an invisible being, creator of all things, supreme wisdom, truth, beauty, and strength, father and redeemer of each man. This goal of prayer always remains hidden to intelligence. For both language and thought fail when we attempt to describe God.

We do know, however, that whenever we address God in fervent prayer we change both soul and body for the better. It could not happen that any man or woman could pray for a single moment without some good result. "No man ever prayed," said Emerson, "without learning something."

One can pray everywhere. In the streets, the subway, the office, the shop, the school, as well as in the solitude of one's own room or among the crowd in a church. There is no prescribed posture, time or place.

"Think of God more often than you breathe," said Epictetus the Stoic. In order really to mold personality, prayer must become a habit. It is meaningless to pray in the morning and to live like a barbarian the remainder of the day. True prayer is a way of life; the truest life is literally a way of prayer.

The best prayers are like the improvisations of gifted lovers, always about the same thing yet never twice the same. We cannot all be creative in prayer. Fortunately, we do not need eloquence; our slightest impulse to prayer is recognized by God. Even if we are pitifully dumb, or if our tongues are overlaid with vanity or deceit, our meager syllables or praise are acceptable to Him, and He showers us with strengthening manifestations of His love.

Today, as never before, prayer is a binding necessity in the lives of men and nations. The lack of emphasis on the religious sense has brought the world to the edge of destruction. Our deepest source of power and perfection has been left miserably undeveloped. Prayer, the basic exercise of the Spirit, must be practiced in our private lives. The neglected soul of man must be made strong enough to assert itself once more. For if the power of prayer is again released and used in the lives of common men and women, if the spirit declares its aims clearly and boldly, there is yet hope that our prayers for a better world will be answered.

It is God that girdeth me with strength, and maketh my way perfect.

—Ps. 18:32

A PRAYER

IF I can do some good today,
If I can serve along life's way,
If I can something helpful say,
Lord, show me how.

If I can right a human wrong,
If I can help to make one strong,
If I can cheer with smile or song,
Lord, show me how.

If I can make a burden less,
If I can aid one in distress,
If I can spread more happiness,
Lord, show me how.

If I can do a kindly deed,
If I can sow a fruitful seed,
If I can help someone in need,
Lord, show me how.

If I can feed a hungry heart,

If I can give a better start,
If I can can fill a nobler part,
Lord, show me how.

—GRENVILLE KLEISER

PRAYER IS MENTAL MEDICINE
By: GRENVILLE KLEISER

THERE ARE MANY RECORDS OF MEN who in times of serious distress have prayed for wisdom and guidance, for faith and hearts of steel. They did not stop to argue about the efficacy of prayer. In the hour of physical pain, of peril, of crisis, they turned to God and earnestly besought His help. And such prayer always brought solace.

Captain Eddie Rickenbacker and his companions, adrift in a rubber raft, tell of how they prayed when threatened with starvation and death, and how a seagull came and landed on Rickenbacker's head. They carved up the carcass and ate it. Prayer, courage, and faith were their chief reliance in the hour of dire need.

We are a religious nation, and as a whole we believe in prayer. Doubtless if prayer had a larger place in our life we would be healthier, stronger, more courageous, more hopeful and better fit for life and duty.

Generalissimo Chiang Kai-Shek is said to take refuge in a period of quiet on his knees whenever he has an important decision to make. Prayer is a part of his daily regime.

An eminent physician tells us that prayer is the most powerful and effective medicine for sick minds. It starts faith working. It cleanses the system of mental poisons—of worry, fear, hatred and the like—and it gives the one who prays a saner slant on life.

Washington knelt in prayer at Valley Forge; Woodrow Wilson called this nation to prayer in the dark days of 1918; through the ages great issues have been met and mastered when God's people waited in His presence.

Serious sickness may be caused by indulgence in jealousy, anger, little meannesses, malicious gossip, or family quarrels. The remedy is often found in establishing an inner calmness, forbearance, and in sincere daily prayer.

In tragic days of hardship, suffering, and anxiety, men are in need of prayer as never before. The pilgrim who bears the cross as he journeys through the night of affliction finds in prayer the sign of victory and the promise of morning.

DEDICATE YOUR LIFE to the service of God. You can carry this lofty spirit into all your daily activities, whatever their nature may be. If it is well to serve God at any time, then it is well to serve Him at all times. If you should use one of your gifts for the honor of God, then you should use all your gifts for this great purpose.

If it is desirable that you should practice purity, wisdom, and righteousness some of the time, surely it is equally desirable that you practise these great virtues all the time. There can be no higher purpose to your life than to serve God at all times, in every thought, word, and act.

It is your privilege to do this from this day forth. God waits on your answer. Think on these things.

A SIMPLE PRAYER

Lord, make me an instrument of Thy Peace. Where there is hatred, let me sow love. Where there is injury, pardon. Where there is doubt, faith. Where there is despair, hope. Where there is darkness, light. Where there is sadness, joy.

Divine Master, grant that I may not so much seek to be consoled as to console; to be understood, as to understand; to be loved, as to love; for it is in giving that we receive, it is in pardoning, that we are pardoned, and it is in dying that we are born to Eternal Life.

—ST. FRANCIS OF ASSISSI

PRAYER IS HOW YOU LIVE
By: HERBERT H. HARRIS

ALL MY LIFE I've been acutely sensitive to odors. Once, when I was about five, I was taken to a flower show. They tell me I stood stock still, closed my eyes and breathed in rapture.

"God must smell like that," I said.

It explains exactly how I feel so often—God must smell like that—that's God's fragrance.

My big sister, Rose, brought me up. I was the son of an elderly couple, and when our mother died, Rose, who was already married and a mother, took me in. She and her famous husband, Lew Fields, the great comedian, raised me with their two sons and two daughters. Rose was sister and mother to me, and I don't think it was an easy assignment.

Because I had a marked response to everything beautiful, conversely, I set out to be tough. And I was tough. I was bat boy for the Giants, and no honor or distinction or success I may have earned in a lifetime could top the thrill of casual 'Hi-ya-boy' intimacy with such heroes as John McGraw, Christy Mathewson, Roger Bresnahan, Rube Marquard and Al Bridwell.

That and one other thing sticks out in childhood for sheer triumph. I was a New York City boy from start to finish, and I love New York like monkeys love peanuts. Up on Ninetieth Street is a tree I planted when I was 12 years old. I don't think there's any other tree as beautiful as that one in all the world. It grew along with me, and I visit it regularly.

When I'm low or discouraged, I go and commune with that tree and all that Joyce Kilmer felt and meant flows through me. Only God can make a tree, but when I was a kid I helped Him put one in a city. He and I take care of that tree, too.

It's odd the close feeling I had to God from earliest childhood. But I had my own deal with God way back and kept it. The Bible lines which I took as personal guides are: Not slothful in business; fervent in Spirit; serving the Lord; and The greatest of these is Charity. But this latter has always seemed too easy. There is so much healing, so many untold blessings, and such great returns in giving, that I often wonder where the spiritual benefit is. It's practical as well as thrilling, and where is the nobility in that?

Well, God and I had our understanding, and I steered clear of all religious matters beyond that. I saw so many kinds of religions and they all seem good, but I couldn't understand why it was furiously important that this church or that creed was It. I grew up of Jewish faith, and revere those who truly practice it.

But the day came—as it does, I guess, with every man or woman—when a miracle stopped me short. The word miracle is one of those that make me uneasy. It affects me like the word "ghost" or "spirits."

It was in France in the First World War. A lieutenant at the time, I was bivouacked in a little village outside of Verdun with eighteen men cut off from everything—news or supplies—while an offensive was launched. The Germans were coming closer and closer; we were between them and the town, and we felt this time we were goners.

Toward dawn I found in my pocket a letter from my sister Rose, which I hadn't found time to open. I read it then. My sister seemed to feel I was in great danger, and she wanted me to know that her prayers were surrounding me with protection and that she had others praying for me. I glanced at the others in the room. They were haggard, scared. They hadn't eaten in 24 hours.

I returned to the letter in which my sister quoted from the Bible:

"I will say of the Lord, He is my refuge and my fortress; my

God, in Him will I trust, His truth shall be my shield and buckler. Thou shalt not be afraid for the terror by night; nor for the arrow that flieth by day; Nor for the pestilence that walketh in darkness, nor for the destruction that wasteth at noonday.

"A thousand shall fall at thy side, and ten thousand at thy right hand, but it shall not come nigh thee."

I folded the letter and put it inside my shirt. I wasn't fearful any longer. I turned to the men and asked: "Did you see that letter I was reading? Keep your chin up. Nothing's going to harm us, because we're being prayed for right this minute. If you guys here have a prayer in you, I'd suggest you pitch in and help."

One man lying in a corner, spoke up with a big foghorn voice: "The Lord be with us."

"Amen," I said, for the first time in my life out loud. The whole roomful repeated it solemnly. I've come to love that word: Amen, or So be it. It's my favorite prayer.

We had barely finished when the big guns tore loose. The next five hours were complete indescribable horror, made doubly so because we were so helpless. I couldn't believe such annihilation possible, nor such noise or smells. The devil must smell like that.

Not until mid-morning did we realize that the Allies were busier than the Boche, who started to fall back about that time. I saw the village church crumple like a child's toy, the buildings nearby in smoking ruins.

I don't know why I looked at my watch. It was 12. "Destruction at noonday," Rose had written. If ever a prophecy was timed that was it. Not one scratch was on any of the nineteen of us there. Nothing in our quarters was disturbed or touched. It was as if a circle had been drawn around our house and barn and the rest of the town wiped out.

Nobody ever again had to convince me of the power of

prayer. The mystery is how people can say prayers matter-of-factly, or absent-mindedly. It's too potent and dynamic to approach lightly.

CREATIVE POWER

THERE is Power within me which is Life itself;
I can turn to it and rest on it;
As I turn to it and rest on it,
It helps me and heals me all the time.

There is Wisdom itself within me which is Life itself;
I can turn to it and rest on it,
As I turn to it and rest on it,
It helps me and heals me all the time.

There is Love itself within me which is Life itself;
I can turn to it and rest on it;
As I turn to it and rest on it,
It helps me and heals me all the time.

—Anonymous

PRAYER FORCE IS LIFE FORCE
By: PAUL MARTIN BRUNET

EVERY time we pray, we are using the Life Force of the Universe.

Prayer force not only releases the latent energies of our being, but renews these energies with vitality and power. Emotional and intellectual energy must be released, or the whole physical system will feel the effects of repressed power.

Notice how an automobile vibrates when the engine is just turning over, or racing in a stationary position. The whole car shakes and quivers with suppressed energy. The moment the energy is released and the car driven along the road, there is harmonious rhythm and right action. Repressed emotion and feeling is just like that and does the same thing to your body.

The Life Force and energy within you is the same Life Power that turns the earth on its axis, causes the sun to explode into rays of millions of volts, and carries the stellar system along with a grace, a sweep and a magnitude that is beyond ordinary comprehension. The feeling of all this is embodied in your prayer.

Daily prayer—communion with God-Power—is as necessary as food, water, or air. For daily prayer helps you release the Divine Energy stored up within your consciousness.

Prayer and treatment is direct application of the dynamic Power of the Universe. Prayer and treatment consciously focus God's healing power along constructive lines. It heals diseases, solves problems, renews our physical being, and charges us with a power and reserve strength above and beyond our ordinary capacity.

"Prayer is power," said the famous Dr. Carrel, and he knew

70

what he was talking about. In his book, "Man the Unknown," he states that cancers have been cured, tumors dissolved and life restored by this natural spiritual means. It is ever at our disposal. It is ever available—if we will but use it with resolution, deliberation and persistency.

The rhythm of regularity is as necessary for definite demonstration as the rhythm of breathing. One deep breath of air does not supply you with enough oxygen for a whole day! And we know we had better keep right on breathing deeply, regularly, rhythmically, or else.

Our hopes, desires, intuitions, and plans are tied up in the deep emotional content of our being. Prayer-treatment releases these deep things of our spirit into orderly sequence and right action. Emotional blocks are often hidden and obscure things which each psychiatrist seeks to uncover—like mushrooms in a dark cellar—and remove. Relieved of the inward pressure—and what is pressure but dammed up conflict? —the mental and physical nature of our being becomes peaceful, poised, balanced.

There is the instance of Abraham Lincoln, when pressed about with cares beyond endurance, retiring to his room for the solace and comfort of prayer. He talked to God as intimately as you and I talk to our best friend. It is reported that at one time, during the Civil War, things looked so hopeless that Lincoln seemed to be crushed by the overwhelming burdens of his position. Going to his room, he talked to God, saying in substance, "God, I've done all I know how to do. I have done everything I can think of. If You want the country saved, You will have to do it. I simply don't know how to do anything more. You will have to take over and run things. I can't....and thank You, God."

It is reported that, as Lincoln came downstairs, a great load lifted from his shoulders, his mind and his heart. He felt free. He was free. He had released his burden to the Power that was greater than himself. Things went better from that day forward. He had emptied himself of inward pressures through prayer.

What do we do when we visit the psychiatrist, the psychoanalyst, the practitioner of Truth? Do we not unburden ourselves of inward turmoils, conflicts, drives, suppressions? Don't we talk things out? Certainly! And prayer is simply the original form of talking things over with Divine Intelligence—which always has the answers, for God always answers prayer!

What more powerful friend could we have than the Divine Physician, the Divine Psychiatrist? The Scriptures are replete with examples of the art and the science of prayer working in everyday affairs. The Inward Soul Nature of our being must be fed, nourished, sustained, by a daily diet of spiritual food. To neglect this is to stumble through life like an overburdened one-cylinder car.

Scientific prayer today teaches us the broader, higher scope and availability of the Universal Power within us. Take hold of some favorite Psalm, prayer, affirmation of Truth. Write it on a card. If you are using a stale prayer, form a new one. Stale prayers and stale thinking aren't any good to you. Get hold of something vitalizing, energizing, powerful. For example:

GOD IS LIFE OF MY BEING. GOD IS THE TRUTH OF MY BEING. GOD IS THE SUBSTANCE OF MY BEING, HERE AND NOW.

Read it. Study it. Get into the rhythm of it. Feel it in every pore of your being. Bathe in it mentally and spiritually. Old things will pass away. New Life Energy is born every time you say it. Think it over three times a day. Say it over twenty times a day—when the flash of fear would interrupt your progress or peace. Why limit yourself? Use it every time you need help of any kind.

Talk to God and LET GOD TALK TO YOU! When you are through with your praying, take time to be still—really very still—and let God talk to you. It will be a new experience, a new adventure, a voyage of discovery of a Power that is greater than yourself. The healing, the peace, the uplift awaits your communion, your blending with the Universal One who seeks to restore, revive, and refresh you all the time. You can say:

I AM GOD ORDAINED—GOD SUSTAINED—GOD MAINTAINED—HERE AND NOW; FOR THE KINGDOM OF GOD IS WITHIN ME.

This is Prayer-force, Life-force, Scientific praying. And you can begin now, here, today. Try it and see. The Spirit of God is within you. "Be not afraid for the Lord thy God is with thee, whithersoever thou goest." No one can take your peace from you except yourself.

God has given His angels charge over you to keep you in all your ways, says the Ninety-first Psalm. As you call upon Him, He will answer you. As you do, God sets you on high above the ordinary fears and worries of the day, for it is written, "With long life will I satisfy him and show him my salvation."

With this deeper consecration and understanding of prayer, you can do the blessed thing. You can claim your good and share it with another, a friend, a companion. Let him in on a new viewpoint of Life and Living. More healings have been accomplished this way than tongue can tell. We are not out to convert anybody. We are out to help and heal, always giving the credit to God. Be a channel for the good that has come to you. Release the Prayer-force. Life-force for another, as it has been released for you.

Now is the time! This is the day, and it will be peace to your soul, balm to your spirit, and a song in your heart as you translate thought into action. Why? Because Prayer is a two-way street. You can think:

IN GIVING TO ANOTHER, I GIVE TO MYSELF. OPENING A DOOR FOR ANOTHER, I OPEN ONE FOR MYSELF.

GIVING TO ANOTHER, I GIVE TO MYSELF, FOR WITH WHAT MEASURE I METE, SHALL BE MEASURED TO

ME AGAIN, AGAIN, AND AGAIN.

THANK GOD! THERE SHALL ALWAYS BE MORE—AND
MORE—AND MORE.

Cast thy burden upon the Lord, and he shall sustain thee.

—Ps. 55:22

PRAYER

PRAYER is the heart's sincere desire,
Uttered or unexpressed;
The motion of a hidden fire
That trembles in the breast.

Prayer is the simplest form of speech
That infant lips can try;
And prayer's sublimest strain doth reach
The Majesty on high.

Prayer is the Christian's vital breath,
The Christian's native air:
His watchword, overcoming death;
He enters heaven with prayer.

—James Montgomery

THE MAGIC OF BELIEVING
A sermon by: DR. NORMAN VINCENT PEALE

THROUGH the "magic of believing," a perennial failure became a very successful man. Of an exceptionally fine family, with educational and business opportunities far beyond the average he also had a tragic flair for failure. Everything he touched went wrong. He tried hard enough. He was industrious and ingenious, but he missed it, he just did not have the touch. Nobody, myself included, could quite understand why. But six or seven years ago this situation was suddenly reversed. His whole life began to focus. Obviously he had found a potent secret.

Recently at luncheon, sitting across the table from him, I could not help but admire this finely set-up, dynamic, attractive man at the height of his power, and said to him "You amaze me, you are a seven-day wonder, or I should put it, a seven-year wonder. Whatever happened to cause this remarkable change in you?"

"Why," he replied "it is all very simple. You will be particularly interested because it all happened through a verse from the Bible which reads as follows: 'If thou believe, all things are possible to him that believeth.' I had read that statement many times," he continued, "and heard it preached on, but without effect. Now suddenly I saw that the key I had missed was to train my mind to believe. So it proved to be. Is it not miraculous?" he asked.

After some thought I replied that I did not think it miraculous at all. Actually what had happened was that he had stumbled on one of the most powerful laws in the universe. It is a law recognized alike by religion and psychology; namely, change your mental habits so that you can believe, that is to say, "have faith," and at once you bring everything into the realm of possibility. This does not mean that merely by believing you are going to get everything you want, for perhaps you are not the best judge of what you ought to have. But it does definitely mean that when you learn to believe, that which has seemingly been impossible moves at once into the area of possibility.

One of the greatest minds ever developed on the American continent was that of the late William James, father of American psychology. He is quoted repeatedly as a source authority for modern psychological thinkers. James said, "Our belief at the beginning of a doubtful undertaking is the one thing (now get that) —is the one thing that assures the successful outcome of our venture." Learn to believe that the primary and basic factor of success is present in any undertaking.

My friend, Dr. Smiley Blanton, distinguished psychiatrist, declares that in his work of helping people, the primary effort is to teach them to believe. Everything hinges on one's mastery of the art of having faith. Some people do not seem able to become believers either in God, or in themselves or in their business. As a result they never get very far. But others have the rare quality of believing—they have faith in God, in themselves and in their work. They become the achievers of this world. Today, men are realizing that the most powerful force in human nature is the power technique taught in the Bible. No book read today remotely approaches it in skillful insight into human nature. If you are trying to live without the Bible you are making the mistake of your life. You are not up-to-date, not truly modern. In fact, you are not scientific: You are actually out-of-date. The Bible is astute in its repetitive emphasis on how a man can make something of himself. Faith-belief—this is the essence of the technique it teaches. If you can believe, nothing is impossible. How astonishingly many times that is demonstrated in the lives of men who become successful, happy and useful!

One of the greatest men alive today is Winston Churchill. What a magnificent figure he was and is. He always demonstrates indomitable faith. During the war he designed what he called floating harbors. He summoned the best engineers in England and ordered them to make floating harbors. They said it could not be done. He replied that he wanted these floating harbors constructed. The engineers became angry, they quarrelled with him and told him it could not be done, that what he asked was impossible.

Churchill barked at them, "Don't quarrel with me, quarrel with your difficulties; make me those floating harbors, I know you can make them."

So they made them and they were an important factor in the ultimate victory.

Impossible! Cannot be done! How many times a day do you say that? It would be a good experiment tomorrow to take along a piece of paper and a pencil in your pocket and every time you say or think "Impossible, it cannot be done," write it down. Tomorrow night paste the result on your mirror. Concentrate on reducing the number on Tuesday; and still further on Wednesday, and on Thursday and on Friday. About a week from now you will experience such an enormous surge of power in your mind that you will drop the concept "impossible" for good. Think in terms of the possible. If now for the first time in your life you really learn to believe, all things will move within the area of possibility. Everything will become different for you.

We all want that, don't we? How is it done? How do we learn to believe? What good does it do to promulgate a principle if we do not tell how to master that important principle and how does one learn to believe? Practice—that is the secret. How do you learn to play a piano; how do you learn to play golf? Practice, is the answer. Nobody ever learned to master anything except by intensive and persistent practice. Moreover, the time to begin practicing is now. Start at once to learn skill in believing, for if you do not start you may go on not believing until you become confirmed in your failure pattern.

To begin this practice simply say to yourself—"I believe" and then say it again and still again. Every day repeat those two magic words many times. Your mind has become so geared to disbelieving that at first it will resist your affirmation in the hope of causing you to repudiate your new determination. Your mind will slyly say, "You are a fool. You do not want to believe at all. Do not let that minister persuade you to say foolishly—'I believe.'—Haven't I, your mind, guided you for a long time? I know you better than he does. Do not believe in this queer talk about faith."

Your mind will react thus because it is not at home with faith. It has been trained to disbelieve. But, if I may so picture your action, turn to your mind and say, "You miserable old mind, I do believe." Keep saying it so firmly and persistently that your mind after a while, with astonishment will exclaim, "He does believe." Then your mind will no longer frustrate you for it will become the ready instrument of your faith. Build the faith thought pattern into your thoughts.

Wise men know the power of the mind to bring to pass that which you believe. The late George Russell, famous Irish editor and poet says, "We become what we habitually contemplate." That is a very subtle truth. The picture which you constantly form in your mind of yourself, your steady contemplation of yourself, is what you will become. Marcus Aurelius said, "A man's life is what his thoughts make of it." Emerson declared, "We are what we think about all day long."

The former president of Northwestern University, Walter Dill Scott, after long years of investigation said, "Failure or success in business is primarily not determined by mental capacity but by mental attitudes."

Psychology and religion together lay stress on the fact that what you practice thinking over a long period of time determines your future. The Bible says "As a man thinketh

78

in his heart, (that is to say—in his subconscious mind) so is he." In the Book of Job is one of the most subtle sentences ever written down in the English language. "That which I have greatly feared has come upon me." Certainly it does. What you greatly fear over a long period of time tends to come upon you because you have created conditions hospitable for failure and disaster. If that works in the negative can we not also say—"That which I greatly believe shall come upon me."

This philosophical truth is practiced by men in all fields. The late great football coach, Knute Rockne, had four rules for determining the selection of football players for his team. (1) I will not have a boy with a swelled head for you cannot teach him anything. (2) I will not have a griper, lucker or complainer. (3) I will allow no dissipation, physically or emotionally. (4) I will not have a boy with an inferiority complex, he must believe he can accomplish things. No wonder one of the greatest coaches in the history of American football was Knute Rockne. He taught football players to believe and his teams gained outstanding victories. When they believed in the outcome the result had already been planted in their minds.

Recently I read an inspiring and stimulating new book called "The Magic of Believing," by Claude M. Bristol. What a great title—"The Magic of Believing." I selected that book title as the caption for this sermon. I am greatly indebted to the author of "The Magic of Believing" for fresh insights and stimulation of thought.

In this book the author presents an argument which Thoreau taught long ago, that the way to successfully achieve is to form a mental picture of yourself as achieving. He presents some remarkable illustrations; one about an expert fisherman who while his companions caught little would pull up one trout after the other. Of course they were astonished and questioned him about his accomplishment. "Oh," he vaguely replied, "I just put the old squeeza-ma-jintiun (his word for magic) on them." When asked what he meant he replied, "I sit in the boat and mentally picture the fish swimming up to my bait. I picture the fish taking the line, and I just pull 'em in."

The author adds a footnote to the effect that the sports editor of one of the great newspapers of the Northwest, who has studied the habits of fish for forty years, says this method is not as foolish as it may appear; that while he cannot explain it, there seems to be a psychic connection between the human mind and the actions of fish. He also declares that in the game of golf if a player strongly pictures himself making a good shot he will tend to do so. A salesman who constantly pictures himself making good sales will attain a fine record.

I tried this principle the other night for I firmly believe in the magic of believing. My wife, three children, and I arrived at six o'clock in the evening at the Pennsylvania station loaded down with bags. We went up to the taxi stand. Realizing it was six o'clock at night when the movement of traffic in New York City is very heavy, I began saying negatively to myself, "It will be absolutely impossible to get a taxi." I even made this comment to one of my children. Then suddenly I became ashamed and said to myself, "You stand up before audiences week after week and urge people to have positive thoughts and here you are negatively affirming there will be no taxis available. Why not practice this positive principle advocated in "The Magic of Believing" and form a mental picture of a taxi coming up to take you home. So I changed my mental attitude by saying to myself, "When my turn comes a taxi will come along for me. It will roll right up to me." This I affirmed with positive thought, forming a picture in my mind. And what do you think? My wife was standing about twenty-five feet from me and a taxi did come up, not in front of me, but directly in front of her.

This may seem an unimportant kind of illustration, but it is based on a solid truth. Condition your mind to believe that things are going to happen for you rather than against you.

Think wrong and things go wrong. Think right and they will go right. As Captain Eddie Rickenbacker once told me, "Think adversity and you will get adversity. Think victory and you will get victory, for the mind tends to create what your thoughts visualize." Even in small things as well as in great matters it is a fact that, "If thou believe, all things are possible to him that believeth."

I have a friend, an important personality. He had a very difficult problem about which he wrote me. I wrote and told him I would pray for him, and urged him to pray and to believe—that at that moment his problem was being solved. Things began to improve. I was in his city sometime later.

He said, "Do you know, the strangest thing happened. I knew you were praying. I, too, was praying—and practicing faith; and all of a sudden I just knew it was going to work out. I found myself believing that it would be so, actually expecting it to happen.

I put my hand on his shoulders and cried, "That's it! That is the great principle. You expected it to happen. That made it happen. You learned to believe. That was the answer."

He looked at me with an attitude of simple faith and said, "That's it. That's what the Bible means. Pray, put it in the hands of God and then believe—'all things are possible to him that believeth'.

If you can just believe—that is the crux of the whole matter. And the only way to do that is by practice. Go out of this building this morning and as you walk down the street practice saying, "I believe, I believe! It can be, it can be, it can be; God will make it so; and I am in His will." You can change everything for yourself if you learn to believe, and you can start the changing process immediately—just as soon as you start believing.

Of course this matter of belief goes even deeper. What I have said thus far, might give some reason for accusing me of placing an undue emphasis upon the psychological powers of the human mind. Do not ever make that mistake.

81

I believe that psychological and psychiatric mechanisms are aids and only aids to the greatness of faith. Faith is a religious thing. We do not merely believe in ourselves, we have faith in God, the basic source of power. Faith is the most powerful life-changing force in this world. We are not changed by our own efforts. You may improve yourself. But you will not essentially change yourself. Men are not basically changed by education or even by religious education. We are not primarily changed by faith in our own powers but we are changed by faith in God. Have faith in God to do wonderful things for you and He will do them.

Undoubtedly there are people who have been struggling against defeating things for years, poor unhappy souls. There are young people here who are becoming aware of the difficult problems they must face. How can you meet these problems successfully? I have seen it happen so many times that I have not a vistage of a doubt that every individual in this congregation can have a marvelous power in his life if he will practice believing the grace of God.

A man wrote me a letter telling how completely defeated he had been. In fact he said that he had even gotten practically down to destitution. He wandered from city to city, living on the generosity of people. He was an educated man. Defeat in the form of liquor and a deep negative complex had reduced him to this unhappy state. He had no confidence in himself, no faith in his ability. One day, so he reported, someone gave him a book by this speaker. He read this book which, like "The Magic of Believing," also teaches the power of faith, the astonishing effect of believing. These principles and techniques seemed to grip his mind. He went to a quiet place and prayed and did exactly as suggested in the book, saying, "I cannot do anything about myself, but I believe God can help me." He employed the power of faith. He believed, and that minute the magic of believing began to work in him. So he writes, "I am now an accountant in this city with a fine business; the old days are past. I have power and happiness in my life. It all resulted from the moment I learned to believe."

Let me say it again—you cannot be defeated by anything in this world if you practice believing in the power of God to renew and transform your life. "If thou believe (that is the secret), all things are possible to him that believeth."

THE PERFECT WAY TO CONQUER WORRY
By: DALE CARNEGIE

I have gone back—well, I was about to say that I had gone back to religion; but that would not be accurate. I have gone forward to a new concept of religion. I no longer have the faintest interest in the differences in creeds that divide the churches. But I am tremendously interested in what religion does for me, just as I am interested in what electricity and good food and water do for me. They help me to lead a richer, fuller, happier life. But religion does far more than that. It brings me spiritual values. It gives me, as William James put it, "a new zest for life...more life, a larger, richer, more satisfying life." It gives me faith, hope, and courage. It banishes tensions, anxieties, fears, and worries. It gives purpose to my life—and direction. It vastly improves my happiness. It gives me abounding health. It helps me to create for myself "an oasis of peace amidst the whirling sands of life."

Francis Bacon was right when he said, three hundred and fifty years ago: "A little philosophy inclineth man's mind to atheism; but depth in philosophy bringeth men's minds about to religion."

I can remember the days when people talked about the conflict between science and religion. But no more. The newest of all sciences-psychiatry-is teaching what the Bible taught. Why? Because psychiatrists realize that prayer and a strong religious faith will banish the worries, the anxieties, the strains and fears that cause more than half of all our ills. They know, as one of their leaders, Dr. A. A. Brill, said: "Anyone who is truly religious does not develop a neurosis."

If religion isn't true, then life is meaningless. It is a tragic farce.

I interviewed Henry Ford a few years prior to his death. Before I met him, I had expected him to show the strains of the long years he had spent in building up and managing one of the world's greatest businesses. So I was surprised to see how calm and well and peaceful he looked at seventy-eight. When I asked him if he ever worried, he replied, "No, I believe God is managing affairs and that He doesn't need any advice from me. With God in charge, I believe that everything will work out for the best in the end. So what is there to worry about?"

Earlier in this book I mentioned that when the judges tried to pick the best story on worry sent in by my students, they had so much difficulty in choosing between two outstanding stories that the prize money was split. Here is the second story that tied for first prize—the unforgettable experience of a woman who had to find out the hard way that "she couldn't get along without God."

I am calling this woman Mary Cushman, although that is not her real name. She has children and grandchildren who might be embarrassed to see her story in print, so I agreed to disguise her identity. However, the woman herself is real —very real. A few months ago, she sat in the armchair beside my desk and told me her story. Here is how it goes:

"During the depression," she said, "my husband's average salary was eighteen dollars a week. Many times we didn't have even that because he didn't get paid when he was ill— and that was often. He had a series of minor accidents; he also had mumps, scarlet fever, and repeated attacks of flu. We lost the little house that we had built with our own hands. We owed fifty dollars at the grocery store—and had five children to feed. I took in washing and ironing from the neighbors, and bought secondhand clothes from the Salvation Army store and made them over for my children to wear. I made myself ill with worry. One day the grocer to whom we owed fifty dollars accused my eleven-year-old boy of stealing a couple of pencils. My son wept as he told me about it. I knew he was honest and sensitive, and I knew that he had been disgraced and humiliated in front of other people. That was the straw that broke my back. I thought of all the misery we had endured, and I couldn't see any hope for the future. I must have become temporarily insane with worry, for I shut off my washing machine, took my little five-year-old daughter into the bedroom, and plugged up the windows and cracks with paper and rags. My little girl said to me, 'Mommy, what are you doing?' And I answered, 'There's a little draft in here.' Then I turned on the gas heater we had in the bedroom—and didn't light it. As I lay down on the bed with my daughter beside me, she said, 'Mommy, this is funny—we just got up a little while ago!' But I said, 'Never mind, we'll take a little nap.' Then I closed my eyes, listening to the gas escape from the heater. I shall never forget the smell of that gas...

"Suddenly I thought I heard music. I listened. I had forgotten to turn the radio off in the kitchen. It didn't matter now. But the music kept on, and presently I heard someone singing an old hymn:

What a Friend we have in God

All our sins and grief's to bear!

What a privilege to carry

Everything to God in prayer.

Oh, what peace we often forfeit

Oh, what needless pains we bear

All because we do not carry

Everything to God in prayer!

"As I listened to that hymn, I realized that I had made a tragic mistake. I had tried to fight all my terrible battles alone. I had not taken everything to God in prayer. I jumped up, turned off the gas, opened the door, and raised the windows.

"I wept and prayed all the rest of that day. Only I didn't pray for help—instead I poured out my soul in thanksgiving to God for the blessings He had given me five splendid children—all of them healthy and fine, strong in body and mind. I promised God that never again would I prove so ungrateful. And I have kept that promise.

"Even after we lost our home and had to move into a little country schoolhouse that we rented for five dollars a month, I thanked God for that schoolhouse; I thanked Him for the fact that I at least had a roof to keep us warm and dry. I thanked God honestly that things were not worse—and I believe that He heard me. For in time things improved—oh, not overnight; but as the depression lightened, we made a little more money. I got a job as a hat-check girl in a large country club and sold stockings as a sideline. To help put himself through college one of my sons got a job on a farm, milked thirteen cows morning and night. Today my children are grown up and married; I have three fine grandchildren. And, as I look back to that terrible day when I turned on the gas, I thank God over and over that I 'woke up' in time. What joys I would have missed if I had carried out that act! How many wonderful years I would have forfeited forever! Whenever I hear now of someone who wants to end his life I feel like crying out: 'Don't do it! Don't' The blackest moments we live through can only last a little time—and then comes the future.

The late Mahatma Gandhi, the greatest Indian leader since Buddha, would have collapsed if he had not been inspired by the sustaining power of prayer. How do I know? Because Gandhi himself said so. "Without prayer" he wrote, "I should have been a lunatic long ago."

When we are harassed and reach the limit of our own strength many of us then turn in desperation to God-"There are no atheists in foxholes." But why wait till we are desperate? Why not renew our strength every day? Why wait even until Sunday? For years I have had the habit of dropping into empty churches on weekday afternoons.

When I feel that I am too rushed and hurried to spare a few minutes to think about spiritual things, I say to myself: "Wait a minute, Dale Carnegie, wait a minute. Why all the feverish hurry and rush, little man? You need to pause and acquire a little perspective." At such times, I frequently drop into the first church that I find open. Although I am a Protestant, I frequently, on weekday afternoons, drop into St. Patrick's Cathedral on Fifth Avenue and remind myself that I'll be dead in another thirty years, but that the great spiritual truths that all churches teach are eternal. I close my eyes and pray. I find that doing this calms my nerves, rests my body, clarifies my perspective, and helps me revalue my values. May I recommend this practice to you?

During the past six years that I have been writing this book I have collected hundreds of examples and concrete cases of how men and women conquered fear and worry by prayer. I have in my filing cabinet folders bulging with case histories. Let's take as a typical example the story of a discouraged and disheartened book salesman, John R. Anthony. Mr. Anthony is now an attorney in Houston, Texas, with offices in the Humble Building. Here is his story as he told it to me.

"Twenty-two years ago I closed my private law office to become state representative of an American lawbook company. My specialty was selling a set of lawbooks to lawyers—a set of books that were almost indispensable.

"I was ably and thoroughly trained for the job. I knew all the direct sales talks, and the convincing answers to all possible objections. Before calling on a prospect, I familiarized myself with his rating as an attorney, the nature of his practice, his politics and hobbies. During my interview, I used that information with ample skill. Yet, something was wrong. I just couldn't get orders!

"I grew discouraged. As the days and weeks passed, I doubled and redoubled my efforts, but was still unable to close enough sales to pay my expenses. A sense of fear and dread grew within me. I became afraid to call on people. Before I could enter a prospect's office, that feeling of dread flared up so strong that I would pace up and down the hallway outside the door, or go out of the building and circle the block. Then, after losing much valuable time and feigning enough courage by sheer willpower to crash the office door, I feebly turned the doorknob with trembling hand—half hoping my prospect would not be in!

"My sales manager threatened to stop my advances if I didn't send in more orders. My wife at home pleaded with me for money to pay the grocery bill for herself and our three children. Worry seized me. Day by day I grew more desperate. I didn't know what to do. As I have already said, I had closed my private law office at home and had given up my clients. Now I was broke. I didn't have the money to pay even my hotel bill. Neither did I have the money to buy a ticket back home; nor did I have the courage to return home a beaten man, even if I had had the ticket. Finally, at the miserable end of another bad day, I trudged back to my hotel room—for the last time, I thought. So far as I was concerned, I was thoroughly beaten. Heartbroken, depressed, I didn't know which way to turn. I hardly cared whether I lived or died. I was sorry I had ever been born. I had nothing but a glass of hot milk that night for dinner. Even that was more than I could afford. I understood that night why desperate men raise a hotel window and jump. I might have done it myself if I had had the courage. I began wondering what was the purpose of life. I didn't know. I couldn't figure it out.

"Since there was no one else to turn to, I turned to God. I began to pray. I implored the Almighty to give me light and understanding and guidance through the dark, dense wilderness of despair that had closed in about me. I asked God to help me get orders for my books and to give me money to feed my wife and children. After that prayer, I opened my eyes and saw a Gideon Bible that lay on the dresser in that lonely hotel room. I opened it and read those beautiful, immortal promises of God that must have inspired countless generations of lonely, worried, and beaten men throughout the ages:

'Take no thought for your life, what ye shall eat, or what ye shall drink; nor yet for your body, what ye shall put on. Is not the life more than meat, and the body than raiment? Behold the fowls of the air: for they sow not, neither do they reap, nor gather into barns; yet your heavenly Father feedeth them. Are ye not much, better than they?. . .But seek ye first the kingdom of God, and His righteousness; and all these things shall be added unto you."

"As I prayed and as I read those words, a miracle happened: my nervous tension fell away. My anxieties, fears, and worries were transformed into heart-warming courage and hope and triumphant faith.

"I was happy, even though I didn't have enough money to pay my hotel bill. I went to bed and slept soundly—free from care—as I had not done for many years.

"Next morning, I could hardly hold myself back until the offices of my prospects were open. I approached the office door of my first prospect that beautiful, cold, rainy day with a bold and positive stride. I turned the doorknob with a firm and steady grip. As I entered, I made a beeline for my man, energetically, chin up, and with appropriate dignity, all smiles, and saying, "Good morning, Mr. Smith! I'm John R. Anthony of the All-American Lawbook Company! 'Oh, yes, yes,' he replied smiling, too, as he rose from his chair with outstretched hand. 'I'm glad to see you. Have a seat!'

"I made more sales that day than I had made in weeks. That evening I proudly returned to my hotel like a conquering hero! I felt like a new man. And I was a new man, because I had a new and victorious mental attitude. No dinner of hot milk that night. No, sir! I had a steak with all the fixings. From that day on, my sales zoomed.

"I was born anew that desperate night twenty-two years ago in a little hotel in Amarillo, Texas. My outward situation the

90

next day was the same as it had been through my weeks of failure, but a tremendous thing had happened inside me. I had suddenly become aware of my relationship with God. A mere man alone can easily be defeated, but a man alive with the power of God within him is invincible. I know. I saw it work in my own life.

"'Ask, and it shall be given you; seek, and ye shall find; knock, and it shall be opened unto YOU.'

I know men who regard religion as something for women and children and preachers. They pride themselves on being "he-men" who can fight their battles alone.

How surprised they might be to learn that some of the most famous "he-men" in the world pray every day. For example, "he-man" Jack Dempsey told me that he never goes to bed without saying his prayers. He told me that he never eats a meal without first thanking God for it. He told me that he prayed every day when he was training for a bout, and that when, he was fighting, he always prayed just before the bell sounded for each round. "Praying," he said, "helped me fight with courage and confidence."

"He-man" Connie Mack told me that he couldn't go to sleep without saying his prayers.

"He-man" Eddie Rickenbaeker told me that he believed his life had been saved by prayer. He prays every day.

"He-man" Edward R. Stettinius, former high official of General Motors and United States Steel, and former Secretary of State, told me that he prayed for wisdom and guidance   every   morning   and   night.

"He-man" J. Pierpont Morgan, the greatest financier of his age, often went alone to Trinity Church, at the head of Wall Street, on Saturday afternoons and knelt in prayer.

When "he-man" Eisenhower flew to England to take Supreme command of the British and American forces, he took only one book on the plane with him—the Bible.

"He-man" General Mark Clark told me that he read his Bible every day during the war and knelt down in prayer. So did Chiang Kai-shek, and General Montgomery—"Monty of El Alamein." So did Lord Nelson at Trafalgar. So did General Washington, Robert E. Lee, Stonewall Jackson, and scores of other great military leaders.

These "he-men" discovered the truth of William James's statement: "We and God have business with each other; and in opening ourselves to His influence, our deepest destiny is fulfilled."

Admiral Byrd knows what it means to "link ourselves with the inexhaustible motive power that spins the universe." His ability to do that pulled him through the most trying ordeal of his life. He tells the story in his book Alone. In 1934, he spent five months in a hut buried beneath the icecap of Ross Barrier deep in the Antarctic. He was the only living creature south of latitude seventy-eight. Blizzards roared above his shack; the cold plunged down to eighty-two degrees below zero; he was completely surrounded by unending night. And then he found, to his horror, he was being slowly poisoned by carbon monoxide that escaped from his stove! What could he do? The nearest help was 123 miles away, and could not possibly reach him for several months. He tried to fix his stove and ventilating system, but the fumes still escaped. They often knocked him out cold. He lay on the floor completely unconscious. He couldn't eat; he couldn't sleep; he became so feeble that he could hardly leave his bunk. He frequently feared he wouldn't live until morning. He was convinced he would die in that cabin, and his body would be hidden by perpetual snows.

What saved his life? One day, in the depths of his despair, he reached for his diary and tried to set down his philosophy of life. "The human race," he wrote, "is not alone in the universe." He thought of the stars overhead, of the orderly swing of the constellations and planets; of how the everlasting sun would, in its time, return to lighten even the wastes of the South Polar regions. And then he wrote in his dairy, "I am not alone."

This realization that he was not alone—not even in a hole in the ice at the end of the earth—was what saved Richard Byrd. "I know it pulled me through," he says. And he goes on to add: "Few men in their lifetime come anywhere near exhausting the resources dwelling within them. There are deep wells of strength that are never used." Richard Byrd learned to tap those wells of strength and use those resources—by turning to God.

Why does religious faith bring us such peace and calm and fortitude? I'll let William James answer that. He says: "The turbulent billows of the fretful surface leave the deep parts of the ocean undisturbed; and to him who has a hold on vaster and more permanent realities, the hourly vicissitudes of his personal destiny seem relatively insignifcant things. The really religious person is accordingly unshakeable and full of equanimity, and calmly ready for any duty that the day may bring forth."

If we are worried and anxious—why not try God? Why not, as Immanuel Kant said, "accept a belief in God because we need such a belief"? Why not link ourselves now "with the inexhaustible motive power that spins the universe"?

Even if you are not a religious person by nature or training —even if you are an out-and-out skeptic—prayer can help you much more than you believe, for it is a practical thing. What do I mean, practical? I mean that prayer fulfills these three very basic psychological needs which all people share, whether they believe in God or not:

1 Prayer helps us to put into words exactly what is troubling us. Praying, in a way, is very much like writing our problem down on paper. If we ask help for a problem—even from God—we must put it into words.

2 Prayer gives us a sense of sharing our burdens, of not

93

being alone. Few of us are so strong that we can bear our heaviest burdens, our most agonizing troubles, all by ourselves. Sometimes our worries are of so intimate a nature that we cannot discuss them even with our closest relatives or friends. Then prayer is the answer. Any psychiatrist will tell us that when we are pent-up and tense, and in an agony of spirit, it is therapeutically good to tell someone our troubles. When we can't tell anyone else—we can always tell God.

3   Prayer puts into force an active principle of doing. It's a first step toward action. I doubt if anyone can pray for some fulfillment, day after day, without benefiting from it— in other words, without taking some steps to bring it to pass. The world-famous scientist, Dr. Alexis Carrel, said: "Prayer is the most powerful form of energy one can generate." So why not make use of it? Call it God or Allah or Spirit—why quarrel with definitions as long as the mysterious powers of nature take us in hand?

"He prayeth best who loveth best

All things both great and small;

For the dear God, who loveth us,

He made and loveth all."

A PRAYER THAT WORKED
By: RUSSELL CONWELL

EVERYONE has heard stories of prayers that brought unusually prompt or effective answers. Some of them are world famous, like Muller's prayer for a food supply for his orphanage; or the prayer of President Garfield's mother at the washtub, when her boy was lost in the forest; or Loest's prayer for money to pay his mortgage next day; or the English boy's prayer for his blind sister's restoration to sight.

But has any of you ever heard of a gang of kidnappers being forced by prayer to return a stolen child? Here is the exact chronicle of such a case, and if it was not prayer which brought about this little child's safe return, then I wish you would tell me what agency was responsible for it.

The possible relation of the law of mental telepathy to this experience has already been suggested and need not be repeated here. But the general sympathy with the parents of the child which was stolen led many Christians to pray for the recovery of the precious little one. At the Baptist Temple some years ago a similar case was presented at the church services and an appeal made to the people to ask the Lord to influence the kidnappers to bring back the child. That led to the discussion of many previous cases where the parents believed that their lost child was returned to them in answer to prayer. In two cases each child was carefully deposited at the door of its parents. In both cases they had held special meetings of their neighbors to pray for the return of their child, and in one case they had appealed to the priest for his intercession. If the Lord used his direct power to bring the child home it must have been used through some event or some direct suggestion having an influence on the minds of the captors, because in the cases here mentioned there was no clue revealed which could lead to the abductors.

But the case I am going to tell you of may illustrate what most probably did occur in other instances. Some years ago, a child two years of age was stolen from the front yard of a home in Charlestown, Massachusetts (now a part of Boston). A large ransom was demanded which was far beyond the reach of the parents. After several weeks of excited search by all the police organizations of the nation the child was secretly returned, without ransom, and left cheerfully rapping on its parents' door. One of the robber gang who had conspired to steal children for ransoms, and who had laid the successful plan to capture that child, was arrested several days after the return of the child and confessed his share in the crime. His account of the influences and events which led to the restoration of the child was a most impressive and convincing illustration of the spiritual forces God may use in such cases.

The band of four robbers could not quiet the child when they carried him away, and they resorted to a gag which nearly lulled the child. But the frightened little fellow screamed whenever the gag was taken from his mouth and would not eat or drink. The child was evidently near to death. Then one of the robbers carried the child to a woman who occupied a room over a saloon in Brooklyn, New York. The woman was able to pacify the child, and explained to acquaintances that the child was an orphan whose mother, a near relation, had just died. The woman knew that the child was being held for a ransom, of which she was promised a large share. But she did not know from what part of the country the child came. She was an irreligious, coarse, profane woman, and cared only for money and drink. But one day she sent a letter to the resort of the gang and told them that she had a clear presentiment that something dreadful would happen to them if they did not hurry up the business of returning the child. As they paid no attention to her warnings she wrote again, saying that she would keep the child but ten days longer. They then visited her or wrote to her to care for the child three weeks longer, as they were sure of the "swag" by that time.

In the following week one of the gang was caught by the foot in a falling window sash as he tried to leap to a fire escape and he was burned to death while he hung there. The hotel was in full blaze when he awoke and his only possible escape was by that window. Another one of the gang swallowed a broken glass button when hastily eating a piece of biscuit at a railroad restaurant. He was taken to a hospital or sanitarium in Montreal, where after long agony he died, and his body was buried in the public ground.

When the woman who held the child heard of that she took the child boldly to the house where the other three or four abductors met and flatly told them that all of them would come under a curse if they did not return that child to his parents. But they made a joke of their comrades' death, and gave her brandy until she wandered home drunk. The child was then placed in charge of a poor widow who was told that the mother was dead and the father was at sea, but would soon return. They paid liberally in advance for the child's board, and none of the circumstances awakened the least suspicion in the widow's mind. One night she slept with the child's arm across her neck. She awoke with a dreadful feeling of being choked to death by a strong man who exclaimed, "That child is stolen, and you must appear before God at once to give an account." The details of her experiences are here quoted from the New York Herald.

The widow called it "a waking dream." She was so shocked by the experience that she would not keep the child and sent for the man who had brought the child and demanded that the child be at once taken away. She did not believe that her warning was a premonition of any crime nor that the child had been stolen, but she was in a state of strange terror and told the man who came for the child that she was too nervous to board so young a child. It appears that when the robber returned to the usual rendezvous, after leaving the child at an orphan asylum and agreeing to pay for the board of "his child," he found another member of the party down with a sudden and dangerous fever. Then he, too, was struck with an impression of coming doom. It remained upon him night and day. He became so intoxicated that he was locked in the jail. In the depression of his recovery from the drink he determined to lull himself. Then the idea that he might escape from his horror by taking the child back to its home became so insistent that as soon as he was released he went after the child and took it back on the night train. He told the lisping child to rap on his father's door and "call for papa." Then he hastened away and did not return to his former gang.

This authentic incident may or may not prove that prayer was answered, but it does show how the Lord may work. The angels of God are sent to pronounce curses on the disobedient sometimes, and terrible plagues are sent on men by them. Hence, the Lord does use various curses to work out His will and it seems reasonable to believe that He does warn men and women by terrible mental impressions. This theory is strongly confirmed by the testimonies found in my large correspondence. Lost children were restored after prayers were made for them in startlingly impressive manners.

At Cape May a fisherman obeyed a wholly unexplainable impulse and put back to the marshes, feeling that he had "left something," but unable to remember what it was. There he heard the cry of the lost child, wading waist deep in the incoming tide. A merchant of Wilmington, Delaware, wrote that his child was taken by the grandparents when his wife died, and after the grandparents died the child was hidden by the relatives. The reason for the action was because of a difference of religious faith. He began one day a regular system of prayer for the recovery of his child. He went to a fishing camp in the woods of Maine in August and his child came into his log hut for a drink of water. She was with a party who camped near by in tents. Another stolen child was the little son of a doctor who prayed long and hard for the return of his little son. The sudden attack of chills felt by a passenger on a Hudson River boat at the pier caused the officers to call him on board from the wharf. The afflicted matron and his own child were in the same stateroom together.

One trustworthy officer of our church testified that his child had wandered away from the railroad station while he was asleep on the bench, and that he could not find her after an all-night search. He prayed at his family prayers, asking the Lord in sobs to protect and return his child. He said that an impression as strong as a voice insisted in his mind that he ought to search in some freightyards across the river. The yards were one mile from the station. He told his friends how he felt and insisted that he would go to the yards and search. There he found his starving child under an old fallen fence. He never could discover any satisfactory solution of the mystery of her presence in the railroad yards. She must have toddled the whole mile among vehicles in the night. He has firmly believed in guardian angels ever since that day.

There were numerous cases told of mental impressions made upon children away from home by the influence of a mother's prayer. To all of these incidents the skeptic will assert that, though there be millions of cases where men and women "happened to think" of the person praying at the moment the prayer was offered, it would not be conclusive proof that the thought was suggested by the prayer or in answer to it. But this suggestion presents other cases wherein it is far more difficult to disbelieve than it is to believe. The weight of evidence is almost overwhelmingly on the side of the religious believer.

The belief that God will so adjust His providences as to bring to a person friends, weather, business, health, and domestic peace in answer to the prayer of some insistent friend is almost universal. General Garibaldi stated that he found that his belief in the efficacy of his mother's prayers in securing protection of his life when in danger was accepted by all his friends as a statement which at least might be realized. The commonsense view that where a theory cannot be subjected to proof either way, it surely is wisest to believe in that view which has the strongest influence for good on the life and usefulness of the believer. What a man believeth, as well as what he thinketh, determines what he is. He who believes in the efficacy of his father's or mother's prayers lives a nobler life than the skeptic. The sincere trusting heart which believes that in God and that man is under the oversight of a loving heavenly Father, is nearer the highest standard of human perfection than is the unstable and reckless man who claims that all things exist by chance.

The friend who sincerely prays for you is a friend who would sacrifice most for you in case of need. Two lovers, separated far and praying long for each other, is an exhibition of the truest, sweetest love. It is, also, the best test of God's disposition to heed the requests of his children. No prayer for another can be felt to be effective which is not inspired more or less by real love. The loving heart is a large part of a great previous character. He or she has an intercessory disposition—an intrinsic tendency toward doing good, and that, with a strong, clean mind, makes a true noble person. Such men are grateful to those who pray for them, and are impelled to pray for others. These are some of the reasons given why people ought always to pray.

LaVergne, TN USA
22 July 2010
190476LV00004B/73/A

9 789563 100259